DAM BUILDERS

The Natural History of Beavers and Their Ponds

DAM BUILDERS

The Natural History of Beavers and Their Ponds

MICHAEL RUNTZ

Fitzhenry & Whiteside

Published in Canada by Fitzhenry & Whiteside

195 Allstate Parkway, Markham, ON, L3R 4T8

Published in the United States by Fitzhenry & Whiteside

311 Washington Street, Brighton, Massachusetts, 02135

www.fitzhenry.ca   godwit@fitzhenry.ca

We acknowledge with thanks the Canada Council for the Arts, and the Ontario Arts Council for their support of our

publishing program. We acknowledge the financial support of the Government of Canada through

the Canada Book Fund (CBF) for our publishing activities.

Library and Archives Canada Cataloguing in Publication

Runtz, Michael W. P., author

Dam builders : the natural history of beavers and their ponds / by Michael Runtz.

Includes index.

ISBN 978-1-55455-324-2 (pbk.)

1. Beavers. 2. Beavers—Habitat. 3. Pond ecology. I. Title.

QL737.R632R86 2015   599.37   C2014-907292-9

Publisher Cataloging-in-Publication Data (U.S)

ISBN 978-1-55455-324-2

Data available on file

Design by Kerry Plumley

Cover image Michael Runtz

Printed and bound in Canada

5 4 3 2 1

to Sheila and Harry Thomson: for your friendship and for generously sharing your vast knowledge

of the "real world" on all of those cherished outings, including many to your precious beaver ponds

to Sloan Watters: for your infinite patience in showing an excitable young boy the ways of the woods,

and for the many years of friendship and encouragement

to Ann Mayall: for supporting my insatiable need to be immersed in Nature,

and for sharing with me its splendour and drama, and at times its humour

CONTENTS

ACKNOWLEDGEMENTS

There are always more people to thank than my delinquent memory usually permits, but I shall endeavour to do my best. Thank you to: the late Jean Cunningham for regaling me with stories of her remarkable uncle, the great naturalist Charles Macnamara, and for generously giving me access to his illustrated nature diaries and unpublished book on beavers; Doug Deugo, George Findlay, Bud and Peggy Levy, Verna McGiffin, Ron Pittaway, Edna Ross, Sheila and Harry Thomson, Adolf Vogg, and Sloan Watters for nurturing the curiosity of an impulsive young naturalist—I wish all of you were still here so that we could continue to share the joy of newfound knowledge; Dan Strickland and Ron Tozer, mentors and friends, for your inspiration and for teaching me how to impart natural history knowledge to others; Brad Steinberg, Brent Frederick, Jeremy Inglis, Jeff Moss, and other members of the Ontario Ministry of Natural Resources for providing me access to remote beaver ponds in Algonquin Provincial Park, one of the finest places for enjoying those amazing habitats and their makers; current and past Bonnechere Provincial Park Superintendents Jim Fraser, Paul Smith, and Jason Mask for your hospitality during my beaver quests; my good friends Bill Crins and Rory MacKay, for

being, as always, bottomless wells of knowledge and advice.

I would like to give a very special thanks to Frank Rosell and Howard Parker of Telemark University College in Bø, Norway, for your invaluable assistance and generous hospitality while I was in your country. Tuk, I hope our paths cross again! Thanks also to Ph.D. candidate Hannah Cross for the boat excursion to your research sites. Good luck, Hannah! And much appreciation to Duncan Halley in Norway for your assistance with the range maps for your species of beaver; I hope we finally meet on my next trip to your beautiful country. Thank you to Dan Patterson and his GIS lab at Carleton University in Ottawa, Ontario, for creating the range maps used in this book; Rosalie Murton, you did an outstanding job.

A big heartfelt thanks goes to Natalia Rybczynski for enthusiastically sharing your knowledge of beavers and their evolutionary history, for providing access to castings/skulls of beavers, and for writing the excellent introduction to this book. Natalia, you are a gem!

I would also like to thank the following for permitting the use of their identified image: Canada Post, the three-pence beaver stamp; the Royal Canadian Mint, the Canadian five-cent piece; the National Archives, the photo of Grey Owl; the Hudson's Bay Company and the London School of Economics, the coat of arms; Parks Canada and Roots Canada Inc., the logo; Bell Canada, the illustration of Frank and Gordon; the Scottish Beaver Trial, the photo of the first release of Eurasian beavers; and Wood Buffalo National Park, the aerial view of the longest beaver dam in the world.

Additionally, I wish to thank Camera Kingston for technical support, Steven Boland of the Renfrew County Public Works and Engineering Department for allowing me access to the Round Lake Road washout, and Karen and Bruce Thompson and other friends for allowing me to visit your precious beaver ponds.

I would be remiss in not thanking my remarkable sons Harrison and Dylan for their frequently tested patience during our "meant-to-be-short-but-were-inevitably-not" nature outings when you were young (Harrison still mentions the canoe outing that turned into a whirligig photography extravaganza).

And last but never least, my heartfelt gratitude to my better half, Ann Mayall, for opening my eyes to the beauty beyond the biology, and for your invaluable suggestions and assistance during the completion of this book; not to mention your patience during those long waits when you accompanied me to beaver sites or while I sat glued to my computer.

PREFACE

For the record, I am not a research biologist who has spent decades looking at beavers, using scientific scrutiny and experimental procedure to separate truth from fiction. Rather, I am a naturalist who owns an insatiable curiosity for beavers and all things wild. The purpose of this book is to provide an accurate, informative, and highly visual overview of the natural history of beavers and the habitats they create. The text is a blend of gleanings from the vast world of scientific literature written by those dedicated to learning new truths, and my own personal observations acquired during the immeasurable and pleasurable time I have spent immersed in the "real world." I have strived to provide the most accurate and up-to-date information available at this time.

A beaver is an evolutionary wonder.

(Above) No other animal in the wild constructs such elaborate structures.

(Opposite) The ponds that beavers create benefit many other animals, including river otters.

Unless otherwise noted, all of the photographs were taken by me. They span nearly three decades of enjoyable effort and represent more than 300 different locations and two continents. All of the beavers and other organisms were wild and free-living, with the sole exception of the spotted salamander larva, which due to its minute size was photographed indoors with special equipment. Captive, human-habituated animals would certainly have been much more co-operative and required significantly less effort than did the wild subjects, but the satisfaction in observing and capturing on camera the behaviours of untamed subjects is infinitely greater than the mere acquisition of trophy images. My preference has always been to experience animals in their natural habitat—you learn much when you deal with wild things on their terms. And there is an additional reward bestowed upon you by the elixir of Nature: a profound enrichment of soul.

None of the countless hours I have spent in the wild have been more enjoyable or educational than those spent at beaver ponds. Beavers are fascinating animals to watch, and even if none are visible when

you visit a pond, you never leave disappointed for there is always so much to see and experience. I believe that if more young children were exposed to the magic of Nature, especially that of beavers and their ponds, they would be healthier in body and mind, and fewer would need the drugs so readily prescribed to deal with the increasingly diagnosed syndrome of ADD, ADHD, and related conditions.

It is my sincere wish that the following pages enhance your understanding of and appreciation for one of the most remarkable animals with which we have the privilege of sharing planet Earth.

(Above) A visit to a beaver pond in any season will bring a smile to a child's face.

(Opposite) The ponds that beavers create benefit many other animals, including tree swallows.

INTRODUCTION

DR NATALIA RYBCZYNSKI

ORIGINS AND EVOLUTION

I really only began thinking about the evolution of beavers when I had an opportunity to work with a paleontological project (paleontology is the study of fossils) on Ellesmere Island in Canada's High Arctic. The area today is arid tundra and the mammals living there include muskoxen, caribou, Arctic wolves, and polar bears. The only rodents present are lemmings. No beavers. But there were beavers in the fossil record. The excavation site we were working on (led by the researcher Dr. C. R. Harington of the Canadian Museum of Nature) was mostly sand with some peat layers, remnants of ancient river systems

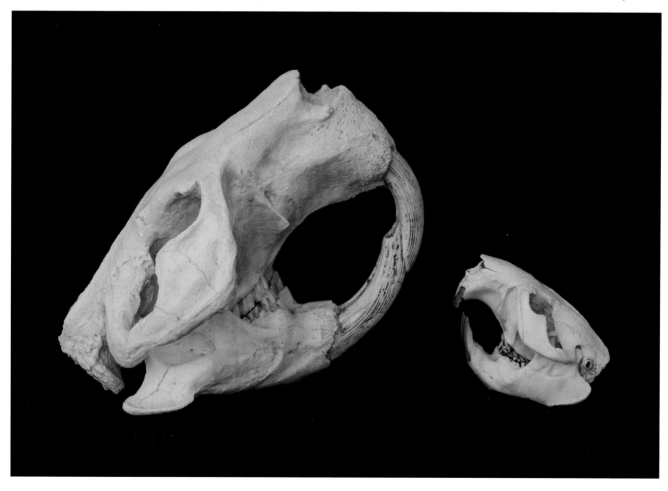

*During the last Ice Age, giant beavers roamed planet Earth. On the right is a skull of an extant species of beaver (*Castor canadensis*) while on the left is a cast of the skull of the giant* Castoroides.

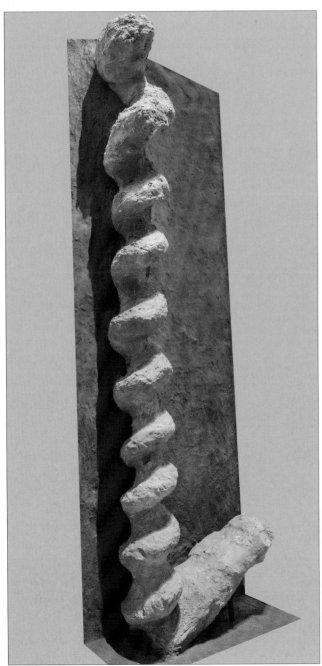

When Devil's Corkscrews, the fossilized spiral burrows of Palaeocastor were first found, there was great debate as to what they actually were. The horizontal section at the bottom of the spiral is the chamber in which the burrowing beavers lived. (with permission of the Royal Ontario Museum © ROM)

and peatlands. We were primarily working on the peat layer, which was over a couple of metres thick. The peat yielded mummified plant remains, including partial trunks of ancient trees, so we know that about three and a half million years ago the area was covered by a boreal-type forest. Also embedded in the peat were the fossil skeletal remains of a horse, a black bear, a deerlet, various small carnivores, and a small beaver along with beaver-cut sticks.

The High Arctic fossil beaver is a bit smaller than modern beavers. The shape of its bones suggests that this animal would have been a good swimmer, and from the great number of cut sticks, also clearly had the capability to cut through trees and branches. And it seems that the bones that made up the tail were a little less developed than those of present-day beavers, which suggest that the tail, if paddle-shaped like modern beavers, might have been much less wide. There is also some evidence from the site that there might have been the remnants of a small dam. So in its general lifestyle, this small beaver may have been fairly similar to the modern beaver. However, this is not true for much of the fossil record of beavers. Some beavers were much smaller and others were giants. Some didn't even swim, using their teeth to excavate burrows rather than cut through trees. So what is a beaver? And what does the fossil record tell us about the evolution of this lineage?

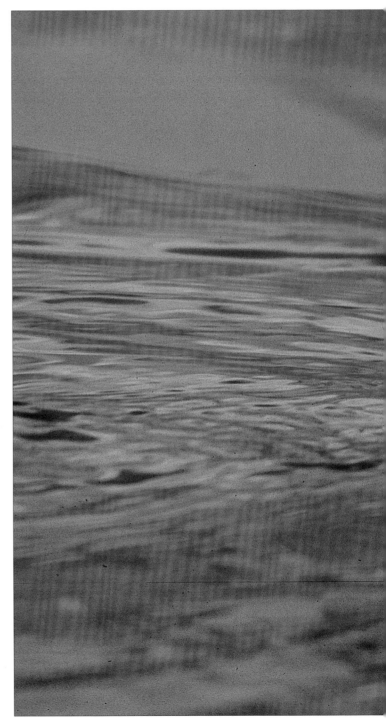

The oldest known beavers come from North America, from rocks that are about 36 million years old. The earliest forms (*Agnotocastor*) as far as we can tell might have been somewhat similar to present-day groundhogs, but details of the skull show that they are actually relatives of beavers. They don't seem to show any specializations for swimming, and their tails were probably long and scaled, unlike those of groundhogs but similar to the tails of rats today. The shape of the teeth suggests the animals would have eaten tough vegetation. From this peculiar ancestor, evolution resulted in two main groups of beavers: burrowing beavers and semi-aquatic beavers.

No doubt the burrowing beavers are a great surprise to those who are familiar with today's beaver. There are 13 known fossil species (within six genera) of burrowing beavers. If you could have seen them alive, these beavers probably would have looked more like pocket gophers, living in burrows in open grassland habitats. Weighing one kilogram or less, they would have had short snouts and broad heads. Consistent with spending much of their time underground, their eyes would have likely been small; it has been suggested that some may have been completely blind. Their tails would have been short, and their forelimbs enlarged with huge claws for digging.

These burrowing beavers are associated with some very mysterious forms in the fossil record. Strange vertical spirals, often exceeding six feet in height, were found in the rock record of the White River Badlands in northwestern Nebraska, Wyoming, and South Dakota. Due to their unknown origin, they were called "Devil's Corkscrews" (*Daemonelix*). These fossil forms were sometimes found in great numbers in close proximity to each other, entangled in the rock like a buried fossil forest stretched over acres. In 1891 the strange fossils were brought to the attention of scientists who speculated on their origins and suggested that these could be strange plants. However, further investigation revealed that in some cases the corkscrew forms contained the skeletal remains of fossil beavers! The Devil's Corkscrews were actually the burrows of ancient beavers. Moreover, with further research it was found that the preservation of some of these burrows was so exceptional that tooth marks found on the walls of the burrows perfectly matched the dimensions of the wide chisel-like front teeth of the skeletal remains of their occupants. It became clear that at least some of the burrowing beavers gnawed their way through the ground!

The gopher-like digging beavers were confined to North America (with one exception being a tiny digging-specialized beaver in Europe, presumably an example of parallel evolution). The situation is different for the swimming beavers, which are known from the fossil record of North America, Europe, and Asia. It seems sometime very early in the evolution of beavers, a primitive population of swimming (semi-aquatic) beavers extended their range from North America to the Eurasian continent. We see an example of this very early beaver in the fossil record of Asia. At the time, the Arctic would have been forested (probably a temperate-type forest), and beavers would have been able to reach Eurasia via Beringia, a land formation (isthmus) that connected what is today Alaska and Russia. Today this land connection is underwater, hidden beneath the Bering Strait.

The earliest fossil beavers known in Europe are of the semi-aquatic kind. Presumably, the northern latitudes were very good for beavers for many millions of years because multiple kinds of swimming beavers later dispersed back into North America.

There are many different kinds of prehistoric semi-aquatic beavers in Europe, Asia, and North America, but the ones that I will focus on belong to two lineages. One lineage includes the High Arctic beaver that I mentioned in my opening paragraph, and the second lineage includes the modern beaver (genus *Castor*). The small High Arctic beaver belongs to the genus *Dipoides*. You might not have heard much about the beaver *Dipoides* before, but you likely have heard something about its near relative, the Ice Age giant beaver *Castoroides*. Probably having evolved from a population of *Dipoides*, *Castoroides* weighed up to 100 kilograms and is the largest rodent ever known to have lived in North America. Fossils of this semi-aquatic beast have been recovered from as far south as Florida to as far north as the Yukon. They died out only about 10,000 years ago, near the end of the last glaciation. Interestingly, along with their contemporaries like the mammoth, giant beavers may have been encountered by North American human populations.

Did the giant *Castoroides* cut down trees? Well, it appears that the teeth of this giant beaver would not have been well-suited for cutting through wood—they just don't seem very sharp. Research on the diet of this animal is ongoing, but the current thinking is that *Castoroides* may have been a bit more like a muskrat in its diet (softer-fibred, less woody material). So perhaps the woodcutting trait, which was present in its ancestor *Dipoides*, was lost in *Castoroides*.

One thing we know about *Dipoides* from the High Arctic fossil evidence is that it was an avid woodcutter, cutting up and collecting branches and trunks of trees. Does this fossil beaver provide us with clues as to when woodcutting evolved in beavers? It might, if we assume that woodcutting evolved only once in beavers. Imagine if we could turn back the clock to see what the ancestor of *Dipoides* looked like, and if we could do the same for *Castor*. If we went backwards through time far enough, through a sequence of ancestors, we would find the population of beavers that links the *Dipoides* line to the *Castor* line. This linking population would be the common ancestor for both lines. The fossil record gives us clues as to what the sequence of ancestors might have looked like. Also from this evidence we can infer that the common

ancestor would have lived about 23 million years ago. This common ancestor would have been smallish, well adapted for swimming (but less so than *Castor*), and would have harvested branches and perhaps small trees. Now, if you could watch evolution in action, moving with the arrow of time, you would see the common ancestor evolve into many different kinds of beavers, including *Castor* and *Dipoides*. From the fossil record, we know that at least 14 genera and many more species of beavers evolved from that single common ancestor. The main points here are that it seems likely that beavers have been cutting up trees for a very long time, and that there were many different kinds of wood cutting beavers living in North America and Eurasia. Think about it from the perspective of the trees—this is a long history of predation by beavers!

The modern beaver (genus *Castor*) is a large rodent. Today the only living rodent that is larger than *Castor* is the South American capybara. *Castor* is also extremely specialized for swimming, more so than any other living rodent, though it is possible that some of the fossil beavers might have been even more aquatic than *Castor*. It has been suggested that *Castoroides* might be one such example. From current evidence, it seems that *Castor* evolved in Eurasia (perhaps Eastern Asia) more than 10 million years ago. *Castor* is an old lineage: for comparison, our own genus (*Homo*) has been in existence only a little more than two million years. By about seven million years ago, a population of *Castor* had become established in North America. Approximately five million years ago, the Bering Strait opened, severing

the land link between North America and Eurasia and the two populations of *Castor*. This means that the North American species (*Castor canadensis*) and the Eurasian species (*Castor fiber*) have been evolving separately for at least five million years.

The evolutionary success of the *Castor* lineage may relate to its ability to change its environment, and to its own behavioural flexibility. Both modern species of beavers are known to create lodges and build dams, resulting in aquatic habitats that support themselves and many other species. Fundamentally, many of *Castor's* behaviours appear to be "hardwired," requiring no learning. On the other hand, these behaviours also involve cognitive capacities that allow beavers to manipulate their environment, using remarkable manual dexterity, and also to respond appropriately to changes in environments through learning. Beavers, along with some primates and dolphins, are among the few mammals that show the capacity to use tools. In one case, a researcher observed a captive beaver using small sticks to plug the three small holes of a water outlet in its enclosure. The animal had carefully whittled down the sticks so that they would exactly fit the outlet holes. In this way, the sticks were deliberately modified to become "tools" suitable for a specific task. Beavers also live in small family groups that require a form of intelligence related to social behaviour. It is perhaps of little surprise then that *Castor's* brain is larger than that of its fossil relatives.

In a way, we can think of *Castor* as the "Great Ape" of the rodent world.

REFERENCES

Flynn, L. J., and L. L. Jacobs. *Castoroidea. Evolution of Tertiary Mammals of North America. Small Mammals, Xenarthrans, and Marine Mammals*. Vol. 2: 391-405. Cambridge: Cambridge University Press, 2008.

Harington, C. R. 1996. "Giant Beaver." *The Beringian Research Notes series*. 6: 1-4.

Hugueney, M. *"Family Castoridae." The Miocene Land Mammals of Europe*. Edited by Rössner, G. E. and K. Heissig. Münich: Verlag Friedrich Pfeil, 1999.

Korth, W. W. *The Tertiary Record of Rodents in North America*. New York: Plenum Press, 1994.

O'Hara, C. C. *The White River Badlands*. Rapid City, SD: South Dakota School of Mines and Technology, 1920. Bulletin 13: 181 196 plates.

Pilleri, G. (ed.). *Investigations on beavers. Volume I*. Berne: Brain Anatomy Institute, University of Berne, 1983.

Pilleri, G. (ed.). *Investigations on beavers. Volume II*. Berne: Brain Anatomy Institute, University of Berne, 1984.

Rybczynski, N. "Castorid phylogenetics: Implications for the evolution of tree-exploitation by beavers." *Journal of Mammalian Evolution*. Vol 14, (2007): 1-35.

Rybczynski, N. "Woodcutting behavior in beavers (Castoridae, Rodentia): estimating ecological performance in a modern and a fossil taxon." *Paleobiology*. Vol. 34, no. 3 (2008): 389-402.

Rybczynski, N., and E. M. Ross, et al. "Re-Evaluation of Sinocastor (Rodentia: Castoridae) with Implications on the Origin of Modern Beavers." *Plos One*. Vol. 5, no. 11 (2010).

CHAPTER 1

OF FAME AND INFAMY

I think it a very safe bet that even if you have never seen a beaver, you know what one looks like. One reason is that the beaver's image is ubiquitous; few days pass without encountering it in some form. I'd be willing to wager (at least a nickel!) that virtually all Canadians have recently had a beaver inside their pocket, wallet, or purse, for its image has resided on the back of the Canadian five-cent piece since 1937. Possibly you have sported one on your clothing or accessories (a beaver resides on Roots products) or, if you are sufficiently mature in years, you may have canoed in one (in earlier times, prior to the rise in popularity of kayaks, Beaver canoes were famous). Regardless of your age, it is highly likely that you walked under one as it sat perched above a door on a school or public facility, for the beaver's image appears on crests and coats of arms galore, including those of provinces, states, cities, and educational institutions (including the London School of Economics and the University of Toronto's Osgoode Hall). However, despite many references to the contrary, the beaver does NOT appear on the Canadian Coat of Arms—which most assuredly is a shame.

If you are a philatelist, your collection probably contains a postage stamp bearing the beaver's likeness, for there have been a number produced over the years. The three-pence Beaver issued in 1851 was not only the first postage stamp produced in Canada, it was the first stamp issued anywhere in the world to bear an animal's likeness! Incidentally, the beaver was chosen to appear on that stamp for two reasons. One was that its predisposition for building dams, a trait depicted on that stamp, was thought representative of the verve of Canada's youth for building new communities. The other was that the beaver's hide, which the animal on the stamp is fortunately still wearing, was at one time the chief form of currency for trade. Thus, the beaver on the three-pence stamp was to represent a robust commerce and vibrant social and economic growth.

As a child, you undoubtedly learned in school about the historic role (albeit a most unknowing and undoubtedly unwilling one) that beavers played in the colonization of this continent, for it was the quest for these fur-bearing animals that fuelled much of the exploration and consequent settlement of North America. The beaver trade was tied to colonization so intimately that in the 1820s Sir George Simpson, governor of the Hudson's Bay Company, decreed that beavers and all other fur-bearing animals be trapped to the point of extirpation in the

(Opposite) Beavers are particularly fond of damming culverts, a predilection that often results in flooded roads. Note the scent mound in the lower left corner of the photo.

Courtesy of Hudson's Bay Company

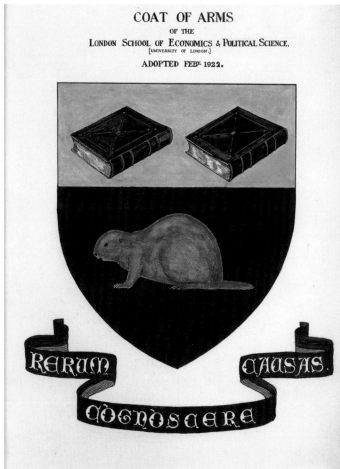

Courtesy of the London School of Economics

Courtesy of Parks Canada

Through the centuries, beavers have been showcased in many genres, including coats of arms (such as that of the Hudson's Bay Company and the London School of Economics), and logos of businesses (such as Roots Canada) and parks (here, Parks Canada). The importance of beavers to the Hudson's Bay Company is clearly reflected in their coat of arms—it is the only animal depicted four times. Incidentally, why are beavers usually depicted looking to the left?

Courtesy of Roots Canada

Courtesy of Bell Canada

© Canada Post Corporation 1851. Reproduced with Permission

Courtesy of the Royal Canadian Mint

Pacific Northwest (which included Oregon and Washington) in order to not only keep out his competitors in the fur industry but also to prevent American immigrants from moving in. Simpson believed that if there were no beavers or any other fur-bearing animal present, the land would not be worth settling.

But if history is not your bent and you have not seen the animal's image in a book, then you have likely seen it on television, for over the years beavers appeared in ads for businesses ranging from building supply chains to telecommunication giants. Ads portraying beavers even saw airtime during a well-watched Super Bowl broadcast. If not on television, then you may have watched beavers on the Big Screen, for they have guest-starred in a number of Hollywood blockbusters. In one film, animated beavers play a pivotal role in saving the world from an evil witch. In another, an actor best known for his James Bond char-

acterization turns from savouring fur-wearing beauties to saving fur-bearing beasties. In 2011, an equally famous actor played a character that used a beaver hand puppet to communicate; that movie was simply titled: *The Beaver*. Beavers have infiltrated our culture in other ways. Young boys in the first level of the international Scouting organization parade in the colours of "Beavers." Winter carnivals in Canada are never complete without "beaver tails," tasty pastries that, apart from a flattened shape, bear absolutely no connection to a piece of a beaver's anatomy. The animal's name has been incorporated into our lexicon in a number of contexts, which vary from ones that are complimentary (such as "busy as a beaver" and "eager as a beaver") to others that run along a very different vein.

Beavers have been the subject of many a philosophical discussion, and not always in rural settings

(Left) From 2005 to 2008 Bell Canada ran a popular ad campaign featuring two cartoon beavers, Frank and Gordon.

(Top right) The first animal to appear on any postage stamp in the world was none other than the beaver (on the 1851 three-pence stamp)!

(Bottom right) The Canadian five-cent piece was not the first coin to bear a beaver's image. In 1849 an illegal mint in Oregon produced a few thousand $5 gold coins known as "beaver coins" or "beaver money."

The ability to harvest wood is a feature that separates beavers from most other animals.

where they occasionally dam creeks, turning farmland into fishless lakes and country roads into carwashes. On Canada's Parliament Hill, the merits of the beaver were hotly debated in the days leading up to March 24, 1975, the date royal assent was given to the bill giving beavers national recognition. 1975 was a very good year for beavers in North America—it was also the year when Maine adopted the beaver as its official State Animal. However, neither that state nor Canada was the first to politically declare its high regard for this creature; apparently more progressive, Oregon adopted the beaver as its State Animal in 1969.

In more recent history, the beaver's worth was once again debated in the Canadian political platform. In 2011, Senator Nicole Eaton proposed that the polar bear replace the beaver in its exalted position as the Canadian National Animal. I had the questionable honour of debating the Senator on national television on the merits of her proposal. I was both amused and dismayed to learn that Senator Eaton's key rationale for transferring the crown was that "beavers were dentally defective rats that hiss [at her]" while polar bears were "majestic symbols of the North." In defence of beavers, I offered that they are accessible to virtually all Canadians, have historic connections to the birth of this country, and are intricately woven into the ecological

36763

Through the persona of an Ojibwa named Grey Owl, the Englishman Archibald Belaney promoted the conservation of beavers. (Courtesy of Canadian National Archives)

fabric of the wild; Polar Bears live in remote regions, and, apart from eating them, have little interaction with other creatures. And beavers are certainly not rats and are in no way "dentally defective." In fact, they sport a marvellous set of teeth that bestows them with power owned by no other animal in the wild. I hope that the Senator reads this book, as well as others that deal informatively with animal natural history.

There is indisputable validity to the iconic status awarded to beavers. Centuries ago when the historical roots of this country were sprouting, beaver pelts filled the canoes of trappers and fur traders. It was the quest for beaver hides (used primarily in the production of hats in Europe) that fuelled much of the exploration and subsequent settlement of Canada and other parts of North America. The drive to trap beavers began along the east coast in the mid-15th century and gained momentum over the ensuing years, hitting full speed by the early 1800s. Beaver hides became legal tender for native trappers

(Above) The early fame of the beaver arose from the use of its underfur to produce hats in Europe. (Courtesy of the Canadian Canoe Museum)

(Left) With its huge, webbed hind feet and unique pancake-flat tail, the beaver is one of the most recognizable animals on this planet.

BEAVER CREEK

BEAVER ROAD 1➡

who, in return for pelts, received a wide variety of items, including hatchets, knives, trinkets, and alcohol. Little did they know that, overseas, the final sale of the fruits of their efforts would reap the vendors a profit nearly 1,000 times the original purchase price of those items. For a century and a half, beaver skins were the standards of currency, and all tradable goods were valued in terms of beaver pelt equivalents. In 1733, at the Hudson's Bay Company post in Fort Albany, one beaver hide would procure its deliverer the choice of 20 fishhooks, 12 buttons, 2 shirts, 2 hatchets, or a gallon of brandy! Europe could simply not get enough beaver pelts and, in North America, new trading companies were formed and trading posts became established increasingly farther away from the coast. Non-native trappers joined the fraternity of beaver hunters, and the network of fur-trading routes branched over the land like fungal mycelia spreading through an old log. Numbers of beavers harvested annually rose from a couple of thousand to a million, largely due to the highly efficient steel trap being added to the arsenal of killing tools. The great naturalist Ernest Thompson Seton estimated that in the period from 1860 to 1870 more than ten million beavers may have been killed in North America.

In addition to their fur, beavers became highly prized for their castor sacs, which produce an oily alkaloid substance known as castoreum. Used by beavers

It seems that wherever you go there are references to beavers!

BEAVER POND
NATURE TRAIL
BC PARKS

The attraction of beavers and their ponds is reflected in the number of trails dedicated to those animals. (Clockwise from top: in E. C. Manning Provincial Park, British Columbia; Algonquin Provincial Park, Ontario; and Ottawa, Ontario).

NCC
CCN

Canada

Beaver Trail   Sentier des Castors

Beaver Pond

for marking their territories, castoreum was proclaimed to be an elixir that cured virtually every human ailment, including hiccups, sleeplessness, spasms, memory loss, and even mental illness. Due to its slow release of scent, it became a valued commodity in the perfume industry, and in some years the Hudson's Bay Company exported more than half a ton of castor sacs to markets in Europe. Today, a number of prestigious perfumes (*Antaeus* by Chanel and *Givenchy III*, for example) still include a synthetic form of castoreum in their chemical composition.

Long before the fur trade with the Europeans erupted, Aboriginal peoples were harvesting beavers. They killed them not for barter but for food and clothing. Bones were shaped into tools: ribs were turned into awls, and inscisors became scrapers. There was never concern for conservation and it was common practice for small groups of natives to wipe out entire colonies of beavers and then move to a new location and repeat the process. On a small scale, this exploitation had little effect on the

Beavers seldom arouse appreciation when (left) they fell trees on private property or (above) build dams across culverts. Perhaps beavers are attracted to culverts because those metal structures amplify the sound of running water, a primary trigger for the dam-building response.

overall population of beavers. However, the magnitude of the relentless pressure placed on beavers by the burgeoning fur trade was another matter.

In addition to opening up an unexplored country, the beaver fur trade kick-started an early economy, and made the primary destinations for beaver pelts in Canada—initially the Hudson's Bay Company and later also the North West Company—more than just successful and powerful organizations. Their domains spanned areas larger than many countries and their governors lived and ruled like kings. The supply of beaver pelts seemed inexhaustible; estimates of the beaver population at its highest in North America ranged from 10 to 50 million (on the low end) to potentially as high as 400 million. They were simply abundant.

At its peak, the fur trade was a major source of employment: in 1799, the aforementioned companies collectively employed more than 1,700 men (interestingly, the North West Company, the corporation that eventually became absorbed by the Hudson's Bay Company, accounted for more than two-thirds of the men). In other parts of North America, additional fur-trading organizations such as the Russian–American Company, the American Fur Company, the Pacific Fur Company, and the Southwest Company were established, and the drive for beaver pelts continued its spread westward into distant parts of the continent. The insatiable greed for beaver furs fuelled competition between companies, and territorial violations, plundering raids, and even mini-wars arose over the valuable pelts.

But as the years passed, an inevitable decline in the beaver population, as well as increased competition

Dammed culverts along logging roads require regular clearing, here in a rather ingenious way.

between the trading companies and soaring debts began to affect even the largest of organizations. In 1821, the North West Company could exist no more as an entity and merged with its chief competitor. With that merger, the area controlled by the amplified Hudson's Bay Company now encompassed a remarkable 7.8 million square kilometres (three million square miles)—an area the size of Australia—making it the largest corporate landowner the world has ever known.

With up to a million beavers trapped each year, over-exploitation eventually brought the species to the brink of extinction. The same fate befell the Eurasian beaver (*Castor fiber*), the only other species of beaver in the world, many years earlier. Fortunately for both beavers, a couple of things changed in their favour. One was that the problem of finding beavers even in North America made the quest for furs financially untenable. In the winter of 1828–29, trappers harvested a grand total of four beavers in 25,000 square kilometres (9,600 square miles) of wilderness near James Bay, a reflection of the situation across the entire continent. With so few beavers to be found, the cost of acquiring pelts was prohibitive. Another bit of good fortune befell beavers. Their fur quite literally fell out of fashion: silk replaced beaver hair as the new rage in attire. The shift in materials for garment production couldn't have come at a better time for beavers, whose very existence had become more than precarious. A near-total reduction in trapping pressure was coupled with legislated protection, and with the initiation of reintroduction programmes, beaver populations in both North America and Europe began to rebound admirably during the following century. Although they may never again reach the lofty pinnacle of their original

populations (largely because vast areas of former beaver habitat have been replaced by human development), in some areas beavers are today nearly as numerous as they were at any time in the past.

We are endeared to beavers not only because their plush hides were once deemed fashionable. These animals seem to be a determined and industrious sort, always cutting down trees or building something. They also appear to be docile and good-natured, living in harmony with other creatures. Hardworking, strong-willed, and congenial—these are the very traits we Canadians embrace as representative of our own demeanour. Justifiably, then, beavers are as much a part of the Canadian psyche as canoes, maple syrup, hockey, and Tim Hortons. Having this country's name reside in the North American beaver's scientific appellation—*Castor canadensis*—seems more than appropriate.

Yet beavers are not always held in high esteem. Canoe trippers encountering yet another dam blocking their route loudly groan their displeasure. More colourful vocalizations fill the air when waterfront residents discover that their favourite shade tree has been transformed into a pyramidal stump. Moans of a different nature arise from campers stricken with "beaver fever" (giardiasis), an illness contracted by drinking untreated water from beaver-inhabited waterways. The real culprit is the protozoa *Giardia lamblia*, which thrives in the intestines of beavers and other aquatic mammals, then gets dispersed as cysts when its hosts defecate in the water. Few accolades are awarded to beavers when they plug culverts, causing streams to flood roads, or when public highways get washed out by water surging through broken dams. In recent years, hostilities have arisen in foreign lands

(Opposite) Torrential rains can cause beaver dams to breach and in rare cases the resulting surge of water washes out highways. This massive washout— approximately 15 metres (49 feet) across and six metres (19 feet) deep— occurred July 20, 2013, on the Round Lake Road near Pembroke, Ontario.

cutline for photos

(Above) A "beaver baffle" consists of a large pipe inserted through a dam with the intake end situated above the dam and protected by a metal cage. The pipe maintains the pond's water level below that of the dam. Another cage surrounds the culvert. With the stimulus of the sound of running water removed, beavers leave the culvert alone. This one is in Gatineau Park, Quebec, where baffles have virtually eliminated "problem beavers."

(Right) Most attempts to keep beavers from blocking culverts usually end in failure.

where beavers have been released for varying reasons. The 25 pairs of North American beavers released in 1946 in Argentina (which historically never had beavers) to generate a fur industry have burgeoned into a population approaching half a million, and the animals are currently modifying the Argentinian and nearby Chilean landscapes in spectacular but undesirable ways. Extolled as a national role model and despised as a destructive pest, the beaver's fame arises from two very different perspectives.

The most remarkable footnote to this dichotomous celebrity is that beavers are not fear-inspiring meat-eaters, like bears and tigers. Neither do they possess the awe-inspiring stature of an elephant or a moose. Instead, beavers belong to the same group of mammals

(Order *Rodentia*) in which mice, lemmings, marmots, and squirrels—creatures that rarely cause us more than a raise of an eyebrow or a skirt—reside. The animal so recognized around the world and enshrined in the culture of our nation is, in reality, a chisel-toothed, flat-tailed, fur-bearing rodent.

But what rodents they are! Beavers own several bragging rights over the rest of their kin, one being longevity: in the wild, beavers live for 10 years or more, with some Eurasian beavers enjoying 16 birthdays. Size is another feature—beavers are huge by rodent standards. An average adult weighs in between 14 and 18 kilograms (31 and 40 pounds), with a few exceeding 33 kilograms (73 pounds). The record belongs to a Wisconsin beaver trapped in 1921 that weighed in at 49.9 kilograms (110 pounds)! Surprisingly, this portliness endows the beaver with the "Largest Rodent" title only in North America; weighing in at an incredible 68 kilograms (150 pounds), the South American capybara sports the rodent world heavyweight crown.

Another distinction is one that separates beavers from not only most other rodents but also the majority of mammals. While beavers spend a considerable amount of time on land, they are even more at home in the water. This amphibious lifestyle is due to a great many special adaptations and modifications to their body plan, alterations that do much more than simply make beavers one of the most recognizable animals on this planet.

As their populations continue to rebound, beavers move into areas inhabited by our species. Unfortunately, far too few communities celebrate their presence.

CHAPTER 2

A GLOBAL PRESENCE

Today beavers are found around the globe in both the Northern and, relatively recently, the Southern Hemispheres. This impressive geographic distribution, however, is not entirely due to natural dispersion, and neither does it consist of only one species. There are two species of beavers alive today: the North American beaver, *Castor canadensis*, and the Eurasian beaver, *Castor fiber*. Each species was originally found only in the region borne by its Anglicized name. But in addition to occupying most of its home continent, the North American beaver has been an involuntary immigrant, for it was transplanted into formerly beaver-less parts of the world such as Tierra del Fuego, and released in Finland and other countries that at one time had beavers, but not of North American vintage.

To the human eye, the two species of beavers, formerly separated by vast oceans for millions of years,

Beversafari

(Opposite) Eurasian beavers look so much like their North American cousins that until relatively recently they were thought to be the same species.

(Left) In some parts of Europe, including Sweden and Norway, beavers are considered to be ecotourism attractions. (Photo courtesy of Telemark Kanalcamping)

Eurasian distribution from Halley, D., Rosell, F., and Saveljev, A. 2012. Population and Distribution of Eurasian Beaver (*Castor fiber*). *Baltic Forestry*, 18(1): 168– 175.

Legend

- *Castor fiber*
- *Castor canadensis*
- *Castor canadensis* introduced
- *Castor fiber* and *Castor canadensis*

Although their original range was considerably more extensive, beavers still occupy much of the Northern Hemisphere. Although Eurasian beavers are not found in North America, North American beavers are now found in a number of countries in Europe, and they also occur in Patagonia.

look and behave near identically, but there are a few differences. Adult Eurasian beavers tend to be a lighter, warmer shade of brown (more like the colour sported by a young North American beaver) and have a tail that is proportionately narrower than that of their New World counterparts. Adults average a bit longer in length than North American beavers (but carry the same mass), and have smaller litters (two or three kits instead of three or

four); the latter is likely the main reason that, in some parts of Europe, their populations have grown more slowly than those of the introduced North American beavers. When marking territories, Eurasian beavers do not add armfuls of mud to their scent mounds, and instead use their front paws to pull loose material under their body before releasing scent. Secretions released from their anal glands, which are used to broadcast their individual

Eurasian (top) and North American (bottom) beavers look very much alike. Although it has been suggested that the ears of Eurasian beavers are smaller, if this is the case, it is very difficult to discern in the field. Much easier to see is the lighter brown coat sported by many Eurasian beavers.

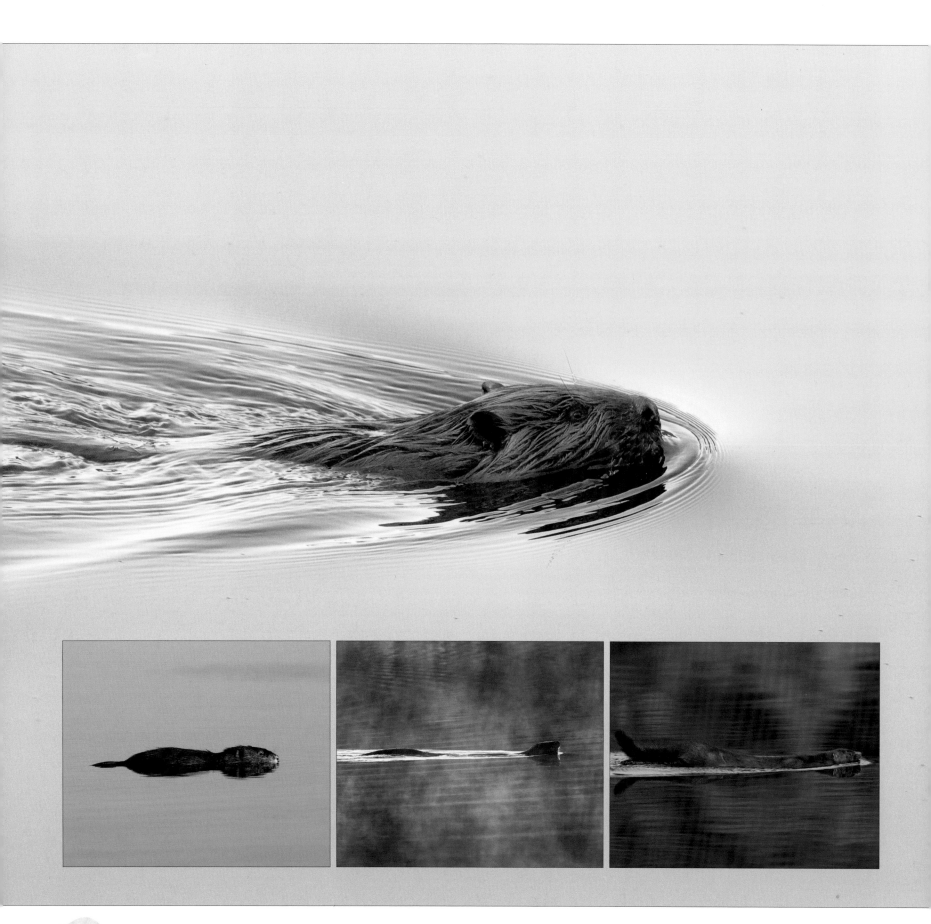

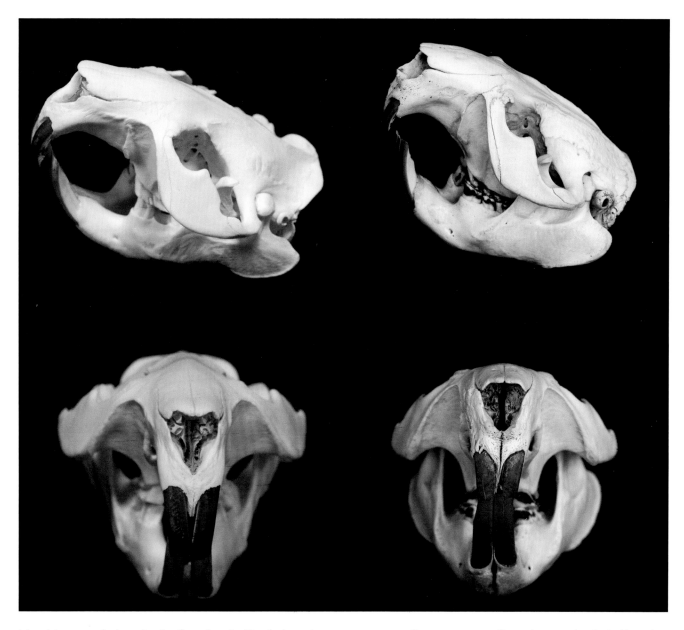

identities, are darkest in the females. In North American beavers, the males produce the darkest secretions of the two sexes, and this species characteristically dives to collect loads of mud to add to the scent mounds before anointing them with their special chemicals. Other differences are less apparent to the eye. The skull of *C. fiber* is slightly more elongated than that of *C. canadensis*, and its nasal opening is strongly triangular, while that of *C. canadensis* is somewhat more square or round. Many male North American beavers have a vestigial uterus, a feature reportedly unknown in their Eurasian counterparts. There are a few other differences but the most important of all lies in their genes: Eurasian beavers have 48 chromosomes while their North American cousins have but 40. This one difference—only discovered in 1973—makes them genetically incompatible; they cannot interbreed. It is not that humans haven't tried to make them do so; a number of attempts were made in Russia were made to crossbreed the two species in captivity. Although the unnatural pairings did produce amorous

Eurasian beavers (top left) have a proportionately longer, narrower skull than North American beavers (top right), and their nasal opening (lower left) is quite triangular, while that of North American beavers (lower right) is more round. Note that other apparent differences in the teeth and skull only result from their positioning.

(Opposite) When swimming, the proportionately large, blunt head of any beaver helps distinguish it from other semi-aquatic animals such as muskrats, river otters, and mink (this one just having launched from a log).

interactions, they resulted in the birth of only one kit and it was stillborn. The genetic difference, the main impetus for the official recognition of two distinct species, gains elevated importance when one considers the ecological ramifications that would arise if the North American beavers currently naturalized and spreading through Europe could successfully interbreed with their Eurasian counterparts. Fortunately for the genetic integrity of Eurasian beavers, this will not happen.

Historically, as their name indicates, Eurasian beavers ranged across much of Europe and Asia, from the Iberian Peninsula and Great Britain to Siberia. Habitat degradation and excessive trapping and hunting resulted in the species becoming critically endangered by the mid-1800s; the last beavers had disappeared from the Netherlands by 1826, Belgium by 1848, and Finland by 1868. Vestigial populations surviving in parts of Germany, France, Norway, Belarus, Russia, and Mongolia likely totalled not many more than 1,200 individuals. The reasons for the decline of the Eurasian beaver mirrored those of its New World counterpart, with one unusual addition: in 1760, the College of Physicians and Faculty of Divinity in Paris decreed the beaver to be a fish because of its scaly tail. This classification allowed beavers to be eaten every day of the year; Catholicism certainly did beavers no favours. Incidentally the capybara in Venezuela had a similar fate due to a papal decree—dates given for this vary from the 16th century to 1764—but it was reportedly the fish-like appearance of this animal's

There is a difference in the shape of the tails of the two species. Adult Eurasian beavers (opposite) have proportionately narrower tails than North American beavers (right). In both species the less obvious, basal portion of the tail contains huge muscles and fat reserves, and is covered by fur.

Telemark University College in Bø, Norway, is a centre for beaver research, with the town visually embracing the importance of its beavers.

(Opposite) After being absent for 400 years, Eurasian beavers (imported from Norway) were released in Scotland in 2009 under the auspices of the Scottish Beaver Trial. (Photo courtesy of Scottish Beaver Trial)

flesh when dried, not an anatomical feature, that was behind the classification.

By the mid-19th century came the realization that through much of their former range, Eurasian beavers were gone. Once abundant, they had become a critically endangered species. Countries began to legislate protection. Norway was the first, passing protective laws in 1845. A century later, reintroduction programs were established throughout Europe and they continue today. Sweden first received beavers in 1922, Latvia in 1927,

Finland in 1935, Poland in 1942–43, Lithuania in 1947, Switzerland in 1956, Estonia in 1957, Bavaria in 1966, Austria in 1976, the Netherlands in 1988, Croatia and Hungary in 1996, Romania in 1998, Serbia and Denmark in 1999, Bulgaria in 2001, and Scotland in 2009. In recent years, other countries (such as Italy and England) have been performing reintroduction viability studies. Not all attempts were successful; habitat degradation remains a serious problem that prevents beavers from returning to certain parts of their former range.

In Europe, earlier attempts to bring back beavers had unforeseen implications for the future welfare of the very animal they were trying to save. Because of the scarcity of beavers, seed animals from North America were recruited. Finland received North American beavers in 1937 and Austria circa 1976. North American beavers were also released in Kamchatka, Denmark, France, and Poland. Keep in mind all of those releases were done with good intentions—to replenish diminished beaver populations. Unfortunately they took place prior to the realization that there were actually two different species of beavers.

In eastern Finland, seven North American beavers were released in 1937, two pairs of which were let go in southeastern Finland where no other beavers existed at the time. The rest were released in southwestern Finland where Eurasian beavers from Norway had been released two years earlier. Lacking competition from other beavers, the population of *C. canadensis* in southeastern Finland grew exponentially, and over the following years it served as a source for relocations to other parts of Finland.

But in the other parts of Finland where both species of beavers had been released, only North American beavers persisted, which led to the conclusion that they had outcompeted their Eurasian relatives. Greater fecundity was one reason suggested for the proliferation of *C. canadensis* in areas where *C. fiber* had resided. However, in not all cases of range overlap was *C. canadensis* the species to enjoy success. North American beavers released in Poland did not survive, with competition from the native species being the explanation. And in Karelia in Russia, Eurasian beavers appear to have displaced North American beavers over

(Left) If it was not for the freshly cut branches, this occupied bank lodge could be easily dismissed as either being inactive or just debris deposited by the river. A beaver-dug channel leading to the lodge's underwater entrance is visible in the murky water in the lower left corner of the photo.

(Opposite) In the mountainous regions of Norway and other parts of Europe, rivers are preferred habitats for Eurasian beavers. Dams are not commonly built, undoubtedly because they would not last long when spring snowmelt and rain fuel surging waters.

a wide area where both species have recently come into contact. Thus, the jury is still out as to which species—if either—is capable of outcompeting the other.

After the realization came that there were two distinct species of beavers and that the introduced North American animals might possibly hinder the recovery of native Eurasian beavers, *Castor canadensis* quickly fell out of favour. Once welcomed with open arms, North American beavers became undesired aliens and are currently considered to be an invasive species in Finland and other parts of Europe.

There is special concern in France where three neighbouring countries currently house expanding *C. canadensis* populations, and the recovering *C. fiber* population comes solely from reintroductions of a relict Rhône River population that possesses a gene pool of special interest. (In 2012, the population estimate for France was 14,000 Eurasian beavers—a hundred-fold increase from the remnant source population.) While the situation will require diligent monitoring, only if *C. canadensis*

Many Eurasian beavers live in riverbanks, adorning the top of the lodge with a scant covering of branches.

Freestanding lodges may not be common in much of Europe but this one rivals in size those typical of North American beavers. For both species, plants growing on a lodge usually indicate a lack of occupants. However, this one was in the process of being re-occupied.

truly does outcompete its native counterpart is there any potential threat to the recovering population of *C. fiber* in France. However, due to the similarity of the two beaver species, the determination of species present in an area is a difficult task, and it must be conclusive if an eradication programme is being considered. DNA analysis may well be the only definitive method of determining if the right species is being targeted.

The reintroduction of beavers into Scotland—known as the Scottish Beaver Trial—is a particularly interesting story, one that illustrates the complications that can arise when attempts are made to bring back an extirpated species into a landscape that has been greatly altered and occupied by humans. The initial proposal to reintroduce Eurasian beavers to Scotland was denied in 2005 by the Deputy Minister for Environment and Rural Development, largely because of concern over how the beavers might affect the Scottish landscape, as well as uncertainty as to how beavers and landowners might coexist without conflict. Three years later, that decision was overturned, and in 2009 the Trial, sponsored by the Royal Zoological Society of Scotland, the Scottish Wildlife Trust, and the host Forestry Commission, became a reality. That year, 11 Eurasian beavers were released in Knapdale, Argyll, and another breeding pair was released the following year. In 2015, after a detailed evaluation of the five-year Trial, a decision will be made as to whether beavers in Scotland will have their landed immigrant status revoked or be granted full Scottish citizenship.

The cost of the official reintroduction—reported to be about two million pounds (about three million US dollars)—was another point of controversy. While it might seem excessive, consider that in 2012, soccer's Lionel

This dam in southern Norway created a sizeable pond but its builders vanished (possibly killed by hunters) so the dam was left unmaintained and the following spring was breached after many days of heavy rain.

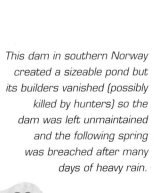

While North American beavers typically build dams and create habitat for plants and other animals, Eurasian beavers frequently live in rivers and share pre-existing habitat with other life forms. In Europe, river cohorts include (clockwise from top left) marsh marigolds, brilliant emeralds, and common goldeneyes (here a female with a crèche of young).

In some parts of Europe, grey alders are commonly harvested for building materials and food.

Like their North American counterparts, Eurasian beavers display a diverse diet. Where available, fresh aquatic grasses and sedges are eagerly devoured.

Messi reportedly earned 27.5 million pounds (about $42 million US), and baseball's Alex Rodriguez, $29 million US (about 20 million pounds). Apart from providing an escape from reality for those people interested in sports, these athletes did little for the betterment of our world. Two million pounds—a small fraction of either man's annual income—was spent in an effort to bring back an endangered species, one that creates habitat for myriad wild creatures and provides immeasurable benefits to our own species. So was that money ill spent? I think not.

To the delight of the sponsors and the businesses benefiting from the surge in ecotourism, the Knapdale beavers appear to have put down roots. But opponents of the Trial were further angered by the discovery in 2006—before the start of the Trial—that beavers were already living in Scotland. Indeed, a small population had been found living along the River Tay but it did not represent a relict population that had been overlooked for 400 years. The general consensus was that the population arose from stock that either had escaped from private collections or been illegally released. As they were not part of a government-sponsored and monitored release programme, Scottish Natural Heritage (an agency funded by the Scottish government) ordered the

Tay beavers to be removed. Opposition quickly sprang up, with one of the main protagonists being the Scottish Wild Beaver Group. Social media came into play with the development of the Facebook site "Save the Free Beavers of the Tay." In response to growing opposition, the eviction order was stayed.

In more recent years, beavers originating from the Tay population have been spotted in other parts of Scotland. Whether or not the Scottish Beaver Trial results in approval of additional releases, it appears that beavers are in Scotland to stay.

The life history of Eurasian beavers in many ways mirrors that of North American beavers, and as the following chapters cover many of the important features of general natural history shared by both species, for the most part, they will not be treated separately here. However, there can be a difference in the way the two species construct their homes. Many Eurasian beavers build lodges inside shoreline banks with a scattering of sticks placed overtop. In North America, freestanding lodges surrounded by water are the general rule and not the exception. And when *Castor canadensis* does build dens along rivers or lakeshores, often (but not always) a much more recognizable dome of sticks is present.

Both species of beavers construct dams, but Eurasian beavers often build structures that are less impressive in stature than those of their seemingly more ambitious North American counterpart. In

In summer, Eurasian beavers typically forage along shores for meadowsweet and other shrubs and herbaceous plants.

mountainous terrain, Eurasian beavers commonly live in rivers and most do not build dams (which may be a reflection of the impossibility of keeping a river dam from being swept away by spring flood waters). Thus, while many North American beavers create habitats for plants and other animals by building dams and creating ponds, many Eurasian beavers share a pre-existing habitat with other organisms.

But when they do build dams, Eurasian beavers, like their North American counterparts, create habitats for other species. They also create a catchment that lessens the effects of spring flooding and helps preserve water tables. In Belgium, the return of beavers has had positive effects on the hydrology of the streams and small rivers that have

In autumn, most Eurasian beavers, like their North American counterparts, create food caches. Birch and aspen branches are important components of these, and are taken from the crowns of trees that have been felled.

been dammed, with the length of time between major flooding events increasing by as much as 50 percent.

Both species of beavers are strictly herbivorous and are generalists, although they do select specific types of trees and herbs from within groups of related species. Poplars and birches are especially popular when beavers of either species are constructing food caches for the winter.

In many parts of their northern range (especially in Europe), beavers are thought of as being willow (*Salix*) specialists, but they are still choosy diners, selecting only certain species of willows as food. In one British Columbia study, beavers harvested several species of *Salix* while ignoring *Salix bebbii*. (Oddly, in Algonquin Park, Ontario, beavers seem to enjoy that species.) This selectivity has led beavers to be called "picky" or "choosy" generalists. I think that "master botanists" would be an equally appropriate title, particularly since beavers use only their nose and not a field guide and hand lens to identify plants that frequently cause us plenty of frustration when we attempt to ascertain what they are.

The availability of willows seems to be a key factor in determining whether Eurasian beavers colonize some areas. *Castor fiber* had been absent from the Czech Republic for more than 250 years. After reintroductions began, beavers preferentially settled waterways with an abundance of willows, even though these sites were much

(Right) The freshly cut end reveals that this pickerel-weed rhizome was harvested by a beaver.

(Opposite) Willows are a preferred food for all beavers in northern regions. In a defensive response to the actions of beavers, willows (and a few other trees such as poplars) produce shoots containing leaves that due to their chemical content are less palatable than adult-form leaves.

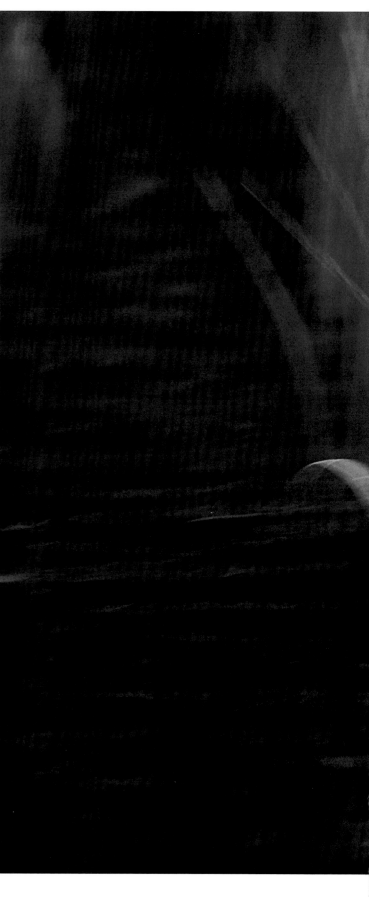

more distant than other seemingly suitable sites that lacked willows. Willows, in some ways, are a renewable resource. Stems sprouting from a beaver-created stump offer increased foraging opportunities, as do new shoots springing up where sunlight reaches the forest floor. The new growth, though, may not be as palatable as the original material harvested by the beaver. In response to an attack by a herbivore, some plants divert a greater concentration of defensive compounds into their new shoots.

By selectively felling trees, beavers can alter the composition of a forest, sometimes converting a mixed forest to one dominated by conifers. Cutting down trees also opens up the canopy, which allows more light to reach the forest floor. This not only benefits sun-loving plants; it could also improve feeding conditions for certain bats, as the removal of trees creates more foraging space in the canopy. Any change in a habitat inevitably benefits some plants and animals while having negative consequences for others.

(Above) Hannah Cross, a Ph.D. student at Norway's Telemark University College, explains to volunteer beaver spotter Ann Mayall the colour codes that identify her ear-tagged research animals, while Jasmin Dawson masterfully commandeers the boat.

(Right) Coloured, numbered ear tags allow researchers to identify individual beavers from a distance.

(Top left) Eurasian beavers regularly mark their territories with castoreum deposits on the shore. Unlike North American beavers, they do not dig mud from the bottom to deposit prior to scent marking.

(Top right) When harvesting food, Eurasian beavers will climb surprisingly steep hills, as evidenced by this drag trail.

(Bottom) A well-used scent mound is easily recognizable.

(Opposite top) A Eurasian beaver climbs onto its scent mound and sniffs for foreign smells. Using its front paws, it pulls mud and plant debris under its body. Its preparations complete, the beaver hunches over and releases its castoreum onto the wet material.

(Opposite bottom) Its "no trespassing" sign posted, the beaver returns to the safety of the water. Beavers will reduce their scent-marking activity if the odour of a predator is present.

(Top) To observe a territorial Eurasian beaver's reaction to the scent of another beaver, a castor sac (acquired from a dead beaver) was placed near a scent mound. After sniffing the foreign scent (and eating the sac!), the beaver promptly deposited its own castoreum on top of that of the illusory intruder.

(Bottom) A beaver's distinctive tail aids in swimming and also enables its owner to quickly dive when danger is detected. The explosive slap of the tail also startles whatever alarmed the beaver, in this case the author!

(Opposite) The loud crack of a beaver's tail slapping the water can be heard in all countries where beavers reside. With their narrower tails, adult Eurasian beavers might displace less water than their North American counterparts when they slap.

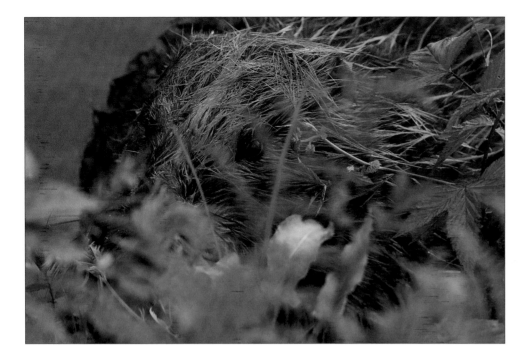

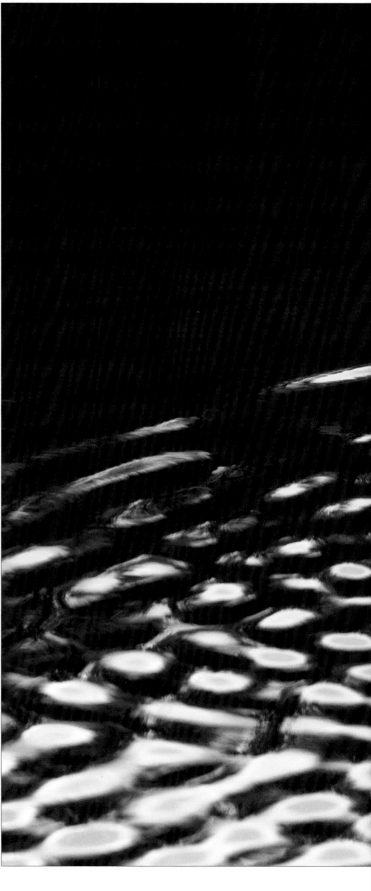

In both North America and Europe there has been debate as to whether beaver dams alter streams to the detriment of fish, such as salmon. Devastation of fish stocks has been a concern expressed by anglers, and an argument used to prevent the reintroduction of beavers to some regions. However, when beavers dam a stream, in many cases the habitat for fish is actually improved (i.e., a reduction in siltation of spawning beds, an increase in the number of invertebrates that serve as food). Overall, the positive effects of a beaver dam on fish habitats do appear to outweigh the negative ones; in most cases beavers have either neutral or positive effects on fish stocks.

While there may be a few significant differences between Eurasian beavers and their North American counterparts, much is shared in terms of life history and their effects on the environment. Both species create habitats that conserve water and support myriad plants and other animals. Therefore it is for good reason that beavers around the globe have been awarded the title: "wetland engineers."

Eurasian beavers, like their North American counterparts, were hunted almost to the point of extinction. Today they are making a tremendous comeback and in some areas are commonly hunted for food, which justifiably keeps them wary of humans.

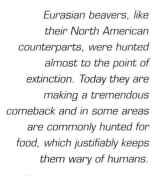

CHAPTER 3

TOOLS OF THE TRADE

Because beavers spend much of their time in the water, they possess numerous adaptations for an aquatic lifestyle. The eyes, ears, and nose are aligned in the upper portion of the head so that when a beaver floats with most of its body submerged, all of its sensory organs remain exposed and operational, much like those of an alligator or hippopotamus when their owner is lurking near the water's surface. When beavers swim underwater, the eyes are protected by diving goggles in the form of nictitating membranes—transparent "third eyelids" that slide sideways over the eye. Flap-like valves close off the ears and nose to prevent water from going in. Furry lips close behind the incisors allowing a beaver to chew underwater without choking on the liquid. Over-sized and fully webbed hind feet provide propulsion through water while a flat leathery tail acts as a rudder and sometimes provides short bursts of speed. The distinctive tail can be divided into two sections: a conical basal third, which is covered in hair and contains much of the powerful musculature that moves that appendage; and the distinctive distal two-thirds, which is oval, flat-tened, and covered in nearly hairless skin composed of tough diamond-shaped keratin scales and stiffened by fat and dense connective tissue.

A marvel of Nature, the beaver's tail is one of the most versatile structures owned by any animal in the world. In addition to helping steer a swimming beaver (a role especially important when a beaver is counteracting the strong pull experienced when dragging a branch in water), the tail also functions as a portable prop when a beaver sits on land, providing support as it gnaws through a tree or grooms its fur (it is positioned differently for those functions, with the tail extending behind the beaver when foraging and forward while grooming). The tail also serves as a pantry for storing fat reserves utilized during winter. The amount of material stored in that appendage is impressive: through the autumn the tail's fat content can double. The tail changes configuration corresponding to the amount of fat it contains, swelling when fat content increases and becoming thinner as the stores are used up.

The one function best known by people is the tail's role in communication. The incredibly loud crack of a beaver's tail slapped on a pond's surface carries far and wide, sending out an alarm to family members both above and below the surface of the pond, warning them of danger. The startling sound is very familiar to anyone who has canoed across a beaver-inhabited

(Opposite) The three main sense organs—the ears, eyes, and nose—are aligned near the top of the head so they remain above water even when most of the beaver's body is submerged.

The tail is used as a third-leg support on land (its position changing from rear-facing [top left] for standing to front-facing [top right] for grooming), a rudder (bottom left) for swimming, and a counterbalance (middle and bottom right) for floating on the water's surface.

waterway near dusk or has paid a visit to a beaver pond at night. The explosive sound that makes hearts leap into throats undoubtedly startles predators; if the slap causes a potential attacker to pause for even a split second, a beaver could be afforded sufficient time to vanish into the safety of deeper water. The unexpected burst of sound could also cause a stealthy predator to move and reveal itself.

Beavers also react to another beaver's tail slap. Colony members become alert and those on land head for water. Some even slap their tails, too. Yet when youngsters slap the water, their alarms often go ignored.

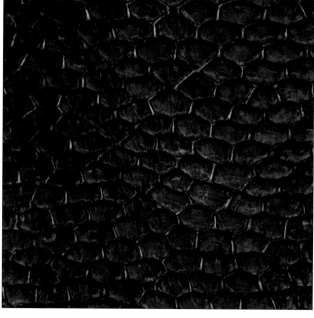

(Above) A beaver's large flat tail is one of its most distinctive and unusual features.

(Left) Tough keratin scales cover the tail, giving it a fish-like appearance.

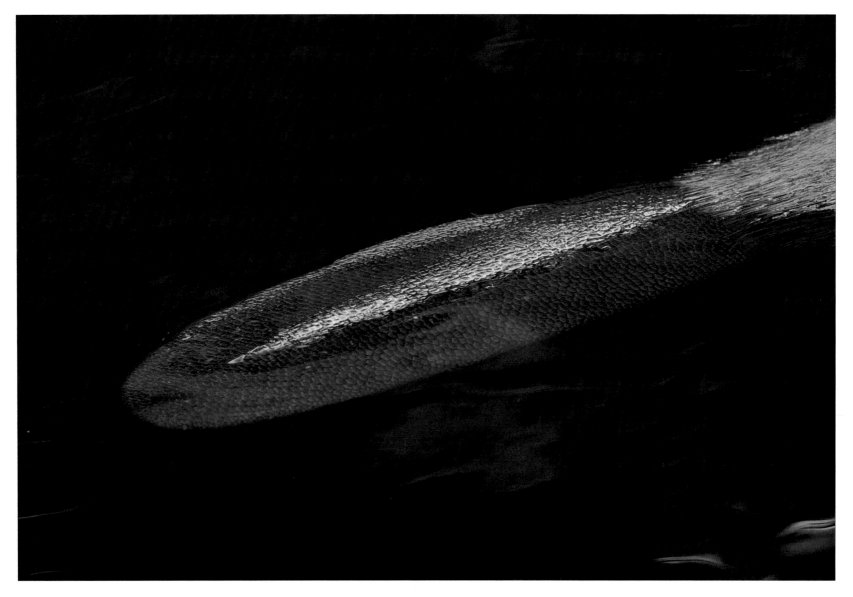

The tail is also used for fat storage and as a temperature control device. (Opposite) Perhaps the most unusual function of a beaver's tail is its role in communication. When mildly alarmed, with its head raised a beaver slaps the water's surface.

If I want to get a beaver's attention, I sometimes toss a stone in the air and just when it is about to hit the water, clap my hands. This can inspire a distant beaver to swim closer to look for the intruder, or a nearby beaver to slap its tail in response. In spring, this action can also cause a beaver to scent mark (deposit its scent) on the shore.

In observing tail slaps over many years, it seems to me that there are two distinct types. Beavers that are only mildly alarmed slap the water while their head is raised above the surface. A shallow dive ensues and the beaver quickly reappears, usually to slap its tail again.

But a beaver that is strongly alarmed immediately goes into a deep dive, its head disappearing under the water before the tail is actually slapped on the surface. Perhaps the famous slap evolved from the tail being used as a diving aid; at the start of a deep dive, the tail pushes up against the water for leverage, helping thrust the animal's head downward. When the tail breaks water, it is quickly slapped down, possibly providing a secondary push for forward momentum underwater. The end result is an explosion of sound and a tremendous displacement of water, events that might serve to confuse and startle an

Anatomy of a tail slap. (Top left) A nervous beaver floats at the surface. (Top right) Deeply alarmed, its head thrusts underwater with the tail providing leverage. (Middle left) As the tail breaks through the surface, it throws water upward and forward into the air. (Middle right) The tail then quickly slaps down, creating the slap and a second explosion of water. (Bottom) As the beaver continues its dive, the tail makes a final appearance, the camera's speed capturing the two water events seen as only one by the human eye. The entire sequence took less than one second to complete.

In a "sloppy" hurried dive, the huge hind feet break through the water's surface, revealing that they too are used for providing thrust.

attacker, as well as warn other beavers of impending danger. During a "slightly alarmed" tail slap, water displacement occurs when the tail hits the water. In a "greatly alarmed" tail slap, water is first thrown into the air by the tail when it pushes up through the surface, with another displacement occurring when the tail is slapped down. Thus, two separate water "events" occur during a deep dive while only one is exhibited in a shallow dive. Of course, the tail slap occurs so quickly that our eye registers a two-displacement event as only one, with all the airborne water seeming to come solely due to the slap.

Of all the functions performed by the tail, perhaps the most unusual is its role as a device for temperature control. When hot, a beaver diverts more blood into this extremity where up to 25 percent of the animal's internal heat can be transferred through the leathery skin to the surrounding water. Conversely, a beaver swimming in

(Opposite) The large incisors, made blood-orange by fortifying iron, are a beaver's chief weapons for defeating the tough armour of trees.

(Top) Beavers remove bark much in the way we glean corn from a cob—by holding them perpendicular to their front incisors.

(Bottom) Trees with soft wood such as poplars are quickly bitten into. Note how the initial attack consists of a series of shallow-angled bites.

cold water can conserve precious body heat by reducing the amount of blood flowing to the tail. To further conserve heat (and, therefore, energy) in cold weather, the blood is shunted through a remarkable net of intertwining arteries and veins located near the tail's base. This net, the *rete mirabile*, functions as a heat exchanger, with veins picking up heat from warm blood carried in the arteries. Because the arterial blood flowing into the tail has much of its heat removed, the temperature

When cutting through trees, beavers bite with only one side of the mouth, alternating sides as they work. (Bottom) The upper incisors serve to anchor a beaver's mouth to the trunk while only one of its long lower incisors attacks the wood. The tooth visible in this photo is not the one biting into the wood.

(Right) For unknown reasons a beaver will abandon its point of attack on a tree (here, a red oak) and initiate another, and sometimes even a third!

(Opposite) The beaver lies on its back to bite into the bottom side of the trunk. Its log nearly severed through on all sides, the beaver quickly delivers the coup de grâce. The entire process took an estimated 15 minutes or less.

gradient from inside the tail to the surrounding water is decreased and, as a result, less heat is lost. In winter, unfrozen water is usually about four degrees C; because of the *rete mirabile* the temperature of the tail can be almost the same as the water around it, remarkably lower than the rest of the body, which is in the mid-30s. With the counter-current system activated, the amount of heat loss is reduced by more than 90 percent. The "wonderful net" benefits beavers in a second way: blood returning to the body is warmed as it flows through the net, and thus requires less energy to raise it to body temperature when it reaches the heart and lungs.

Counter-current heat exchangers are also found in a beaver's hind legs, so the huge hind feet function in a similar way. These remarkable systems are not unique to beavers, however. Their presence in ducks, otters, and gulls, to name but a few, is the reason they, like beavers,

can stand on ice or swim in frigid water without their legs and feet becoming frozen.

Most of a beaver's warmth comes from its luxurious fur coat, one that has adorned many a head and torso of our species through the centuries. Long, thick, flattened hairs comprise the visible portion of the coat. Under the guard hairs and next to the skin lies a woolly layer of short, thick grey underfur. These hairs bear barb-like projections that hook the hairs together, helping to trap air next to the skin, which keeps beavers warm in much the same manner thermal underwear functions to keep us cosy in winter. The density of the hairs—there can be more than 20,000 per square centimetre—along with the trapped air form an additional barrier against water, and may also help to keep beavers afloat. Incidentally, it was only the thick underfur that was used in the

Trees of this stature are usually exploited only when they grow next to the safety of water.

production of beaver hats. To make their beaver pelts more valuable for trade, natives would make coats from beavers' hides, and then wear them inside out until the long guard hairs fell out.

A beaver's hair coat readily sheds water, which suggests that it is waterproofed. It has been long thought that substances released by the paired anal glands, and possibly even the castor sacs, were involved. The anal glands do release an oily substance and it is released via papillae that extrude through the cloaca, the chamber that also receives the offerings of the digestive, urinary, and reproductive tracts. When North American beavers groom, they sit upright with their tail stuck out in front of the body, a position that appears to expose the cloacal opening. They frequently rub their dexterous front hands in the general area of the cloacal region before vigorously working them through the fur. Thus, anal gland secretions would seem to be a likely candidate for the source of waterproofing compounds. This has been generally accepted to be the case and is reported as fact through much of the literature about beavers.

However, the evidence that anal gland products are used to waterproof a beaver's coat seems, to date, to be only circumstantial, such as: the hair reportedly having decreased ability to shed water when anal glands are deactivated, and a baby beaver's fur not being water-proof until after its anal glands mature. Moreover, in Eurasian beavers there has been compelling evidence that anal gland secretions are not used to waterproof a beaver's fur. Frank Rosell at Telemark University College examined the fur of almost two dozen Eurasian beavers to see if they applied castoreum from the castor sacs and/or oil from the anal glands to their hair. He found no

castoreum present in any of the samples he examined. The big surprise was that there were anal gland secretions present on only 13 percent of the beavers, and on those it was found only around the cloaca, which was not unexpected because that is where these compounds are released after physical stimulation of the papillae. What Rosell did find on all hair samples, regardless of location on the beavers, was the lipid squalene, an organic compound released by skin glands. Twenty-four years before Rosell's discovery, University of Iowa medical researchers Lindholm and Downing found squalene to be present in the fur of North American beavers. Interestingly, they also found squalene to be present in the hair of river otters, another semi-aquatic mammal. (Oddly, they also found squalene in the hair of a non-aquatic, arboreal mammal; however, that species eats juicy fruit, so water-proofed hair could be an advantage for it, too.) Is squalene the compound that North American beavers

Beavers appear to have a limited ability to climb.

The remarkable flexibility of a beaver is apparent during grooming sessions. If a beaver's facial expression is any indication, grooming might also be a pleasurable experience.

spread through their fur when they groom, and not oils released by the anal glands? Does the "tail forward" position of North American beavers simply enhance the flexibility and use of their hind legs, whose feet contain a special grooming claw that is applied to the upper body regions during grooming sessions? Is squalene more easily accessed from the belly above the cloaca, a location that North American beavers seem to give a lot of attention to when they groom? Or are North American beavers different from Eurasian beavers in that they do use anal gland secretions to waterproof their hair? Obviously the waterproofing issue is not yet fully resolved, and there is need for further research.

During grooming sessions, a most unusual hair-dressing tool is employed. Each hind foot's second innermost toe is equipped with a large "split" toenail. The nail is not really split but gives that appearance because a regular nail sits atop a hard, leathery secondary nail. The innermost toe also sports a less developed version of that nail. With dexterity that would make any NHL goaltender envious, a beaver can raise its leg so that the hind foot reaches the back of its head, enabling the comb to groom that part of the body. The double nail, which appears capable of being spread open or closed like a clam shell, might clear up tangled hair, or remove undesired passengers, such as mites and ticks; it has even been suggested that the unusual nail is used to squeeze water from the hair. Beavers frequently groom alone but mutual grooming between family members occurs regularly, especially inside the cramped lodge.

A beaver's body displays a rather interesting shape. River otters, aquatic weasels that slip through the water with the speed and agility of Michael Phelps, own

elongated streamlined bodies. Thus, the rotund body of a beaver might have you think that those animals move through the water with the ease of a barge. Although not slim, a beaver's body is no liability when it comes to swimming, for its shape is actually that of a teardrop, a form that makes its owner every bit as streamlined as a seal. The shape reflects a compromise between two

needs: beavers need to swim and dive efficiently, and they need to drag heavy chunks of wood over land and through water. For pulling heavy loads, beavers possess extremely large and powerful neck and head muscles that render beavers the Rottweilers of the rodent world. And these muscles take up space, hence the enlarged upper torso of a beaver. There is another benefit to having a portly body plan: long, thin animals tend to lose more heat relative to their body size than do plump animals of the same weight. Thus, a beaver's shape helps conserve heat during winter, a time when these animals are far less active than otters.

With its full figure, a beaver will never set an Olympic swimming record—top speed is around eight kilometres (five miles) per hour—but what is lost in speed is more than made up for in endurance. Beavers are marathoners capable of traversing large lakes several times a night. They are also superb divers that remain underwater for

(Above) Colony members often partake in mutual grooming both inside and outside the lodge.

(Opposite) The two innermost toes on each hind foot contain a special double nail used for grooming. This unusual feature is most developed on the second innermost toe.

Whether in shallow water or on land, beavers regularly stand up to sniff the air for danger.

remarkable lengths of time. A number of features endow beavers with this ability. Nose and ear valves shut to keep out water during dives. When a beaver refills its lungs, 75 percent of the air is replaced, a highly efficient exchange of air that is nothing less than magnificent when compared to our paltry 15 percent. The exchange provides a rich supply of oxygen to the blood and the oversized liver, which acts like an internal scuba tank. The use of oxygen is made frugal underwater by a diving reflex that slows the heart rate to about 60 beats per minute—nearly half the rate exhibited by a swimming beaver. Special nerves in the

nose and mouth initiate this "diving reflex," which also sends more blood to the brain, heart, and larger muscles while reducing the flow to the extremities. Equipped with these adaptations, a beaver can remain underwater up to 15 minutes—an astonishing feat that would have put Houdini to shame. However, most beavers do not push their ability to the limit, and surface for air after only five or six minutes. When a beaver swims underwater, the trail of rising bubbles (some escaping from the thick guard hairs, others released during exhalation) allows you to follow the animal's movements, on occasion even under clear ice.

Smell is a beaver's main sense.

The water is a beaver's sanctuary and even when food is harvested on land, it is usually dragged to the water before being enjoyed. This type of foraging—going out in all directions from a specific place (the pond) and returning to eat there—is called "central foraging." Beavers are best known for devouring the bark of trees, but they also eat twigs and leaves, ferns, newly sprouted grasses and sedges, and the roots and tubers of many plants. When available, aquatic plants such as water-lilies and water-shield form an important part of the diet, with the bottom-lying rhizomes of yellow pond-lilies being particularly savoured. Most food is eaten in shallow water near the shore or on top of rocks, half-submerged logs, or platforms of mud, cattail mats, or floating peat. Inedible portions of food generously adorn favoured "feeding beds," making them easily recognizable. Aquatic plants are also devoured while the beaver floats on the water's surface. Indeed, one of the best ways to find beavers in summer is to look in late evening for ripples among the floating leaves of aquatic plants.

In northern regions, beavers experience a reduction in activity in winter but, because they do not hibernate, they must eat. However, the ice barrier on top of the frigid waterway and deep snow on the land provide substantial obstacles to getting fresh food. Beavers have brilliantly solved this problem by creating a winter larder known as a food pile, which is situated near the lodge. Access is achieved by swimming under the ice, and branches are either pulled or cut from the pile and brought back into the lodge to be eaten. Interestingly, most of the food is apparently consumed by the colony's youngest beavers, who continue to grow through this season, while the adults experience a significant loss in weight. The food

pile is created in the fall and beavers expend a lot of energy making it, working well into the day, especially just before the pond becomes locked in ice. However, not always is a food cache created. If the water remains unfrozen, beavers sometimes forgo the stash. It has also been reported that access to a rich supply of submerged rhizomes can result in an absence of stored food.

Whether eaten in winter or summer, plant tissues, particularly the bark and wood of trees, are difficult to digest due to the tough structural component, cellulose. Like many other herbivores, beavers do not produce the enzyme cellulase that digests cellulose, so they enlist the aid of microorganisms to do the initial digestion for them. Bacteria inhabiting the intestinal tract provide this service but because they, unlike the bacteria in the stomach rumen of deer and moose, are situated quite far down the digestive system in an incredibly long (70 percent of body length) intestinal sac called a caecum, the waste products are still high in food value when they leave the body. Being thrifty animals, beavers reclaim the unused nutrients in a fashion that may seem somewhat unsavoury—they eat their droppings. With less than

(Above) Water is a beaver's sanctuary, allowing it to groom and eat in safety.

(Opposite) Trembling aspens are favourite meals and entire tracts of these trees are sometimes felled in the autumn when winter food caches are being made.

(Right) Even while eating, a beaver smells its food, seemingly to confirm its edibility.

(Below) The long facial whiskers known as vibrissae are sensitive to touch.

10 percent of the bark's nutritional content digested on the first pass through the body but reportedly up to 90 percent after the second pass, it is clear that beavers depend heavily on their symbiotic partners for nutrition. Coprophagy, the art of eating one's faecal deposits, is not unique to beavers; rabbits and hares conserve nutrients in a similar fashion. After the first bacterial treatment, which takes around 11 hours, the droppings are black and paste-like. When they exit after the second pass, which takes about two days, they are brown and pellet-like.

On a beaver's grocery list, poplars (especially trembling aspen) and willows reside at the top, with white birch and dogwoods also given an elevated position.

While beavers are known as generalist herbivores, they preferentially select foods. For example, when a diversity of willows is found in one location, beavers will cut down only certain species while ignoring others. As preferred tree species become depleted, they turn to those offering less nutrition, such as red maples and spruce and other types of coniferous trees.

Upon seeing a dozen speckled alders cut down, it is easy to jump to the conclusion that beavers enjoy eating that species of shrub. However, beavers harvest trees and shrubs not just for food. They often cut less palatable species such as speckled alder for use as building materials, or ballast to hold down more edible items in a winter food pile. Only after direct observation of an animal eating a plant, examination of leftovers at a feeding bed, or analysis of stomach contents and faeces can conclusions concerning dietary choices of beavers be safely made.

There are many factors that determine what types of food a beaver selects. The amount of nutrition and energy acquired from a plant differs from species to species, as does the difficulty the plant presents in being

What this beaver is doing with its foot while floating on its back is anyone's guess. This posture may be behind imaginative speculation that beavers use their grooming claws to remove wood splinters from their teeth.

processed externally as well as internally. The amounts of lignin and fibre in the tissues are factors that affect how long it takes a beaver to eat a meal and later void its waste products. For example, the stems and leaves of water-lilies are soft tissues that are quickly consumed and digested, and beavers can eat a lot of this material in a relatively short period of time. But those tissues do not supply as much energy as does, say, the bark of trembling aspen, which has a greater degree of physical fortification and, thus, takes a much longer time to process. Aquatic plants however, contain much higher levels of sodium than do aspens; they offer more crude protein and are acquired with very little expenditure of energy. Therefore, they remain a favoured food of beavers. Trembling aspen wood is more easily chewed and digested than that of speckled alder or red maple, and offers a higher nutritional return in terms of energy than either of them. It makes sense, then, that when available, aspen is a beaver's preferred tree. Beavers have been shown to be resourceful in the

The majority of meals are consumed in the safety of the water. Twigs and small branches are completely consumed.

way they select food resources, choosing to get the best return for their efforts. John Fryxell at Guelph University in Ontario and Dietland Müller-Schwarze at the State University of New York College of Environmental Science and Forestry have conducted fascinating research on the dietary choices of beavers.

Wood requires special tools for processing and beavers certainly own the right equipment. Their four oversized incisors never stop growing but this poses little problem, for they constantly wear as they are used. Those teeth also continuously self-sharpen. Because the thin coat of enamel (orange due to its fortifying iron) on the outer surface is harder than the white dentine it overlies, the incisors wear more quickly on their inner surface. This results in a sharp chisel shape, perfect for defeating

(Above) Bark of select trees such as trembling aspen and certain willows is an important food, especially from autumn through to spring.

(Left) In late spring and summer, beavers eat a lot of herbaceous material and small shrubs, including the leaves and stems of raspberries.

Long thin sticks are sometimes cut in two, with both halves being simultaneously devoured.

the woody armour of trees. Between these cutting tools and the flat cheek teeth, which bear convoluted ridges for grinding and shredding, lies a large gap called the diastema. A beaver's fleshy, furred lips can close in this gap, enabling the animal to chew through branches while its mouth is functionally closed. This feature allows beavers to chomp through trees without choking on wood chips and, along with a stopper formed by the epiglottis and part of the tongue, to chew underwater without drowning. Beavers apparently breathe only through their nose, another feature useful for underwater dining.

Beavers employ two different techniques when biting into wood. When dining, beavers hold branches with their front feet and bite off the bark with their front teeth positioned perpendicular to the sticks, similar to the way we use our incisors to strip kernels off corn cobs. But when felling trees or chewing through large branches, beavers typically bite with one side of their mouth, periodically alternating sides as they work through the wood. The two 45° angled bites (combining to produce a 90° cut) provide more force and thus a more efficient cut, much in the way chopping with alternating angles

This beaver is eating clusters of white pine needles, a most unusual food. It is likely a red squirrel nipped the needle clusters from the tree, which overhung the pond, and this beaver came across them floating in the water.

Aquatic plants, such as water-lilies, form a large part of a beaver's summer diet. All parts—stems, leaves, rhizomes, and flowers—are consumed. Although low in certain nutrients, aquatic plants contain a lot of sodium, and some of their chemical defence compounds are used by beavers as components of castoreum.

makes an axe bite more quickly through a log. When biting into wood, the upper incisors anchor the head while the lower incisors, powered by massive temporalis muscles, slice into the wood, with only one tooth actually making contact with each bite.

With felled trees lying haphazardly on the ground and some hung up in the crowns of others, a forest worked on by beavers can easily give the impression that the animals indiscriminately cut everything in sight. But in reality they do not, and studies have shown that there is method to their apparent madness. Beavers select not only certain species of trees, but also certain ages and sizes. Like all animals, beavers face constraints on their foraging behaviour. Larger trees take more time and effort to fell

than smaller trees. As the weight of a tree and its distance from water increases, so does the amount of energy and time required to get it to the water. The more time a beaver spends out of water, the greater its risk of being killed by a predator. All of these considerations have forced beavers to obtain food in a manner ecologists call "optimal foraging," which simply means that the animals feed in a fashion that gives them the best nutritional return for the degree of risk and investment of energy. Generally the trees that entice beavers to travel the greatest distances from water are those that offer the highest nutritional value and bear small girths. Smaller trees are faster to cut and easier to pull, which means not only expending less energy when harvesting them but also returning to the safety of water

Young beavers often roll water-lily leaves into "wraps."

(Top) A beaver's tail sticking out of shallow water is a sure sign the animal is gathering rhizomes from the bottom of the pond.

(Bottom) The flowers of yellow pond-lilies are not only spectacular but are also eaten by beavers.

(Opposite) Beavers eat the basal portions of cattails and particularly enjoy the rhizomes of yellow pond-lilies, which can reach colossal size.

more quickly. The distance between a food resource and the water is an important factor; numerous studies have revealed that most beaver harvesting occurs not much more than 60 metres (200 feet) from their aquatic safety net.

Frequently, one comes across large trees that were felled and apparently abandoned and wasted. The odds are high, however, that the branches forming the crowns of those trees have been removed and taken back to the pond. That is unless, of course, the tree got hung up in the crown of an adjacent tree; in that case it had gone to waste. On rare occasions a tree falls on a beaver that failed to get out of its way (when the tree starts to fall the beaver usually scampers back to the water). A friend

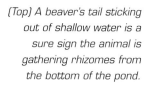

once told me about coming across a dead beaver pinned by its tail under a felled tree. The ground had been extensively torn up in an arc around the beaver, reflecting both the magnitude and the futility of its efforts to escape.

Beavers are not built for scaling cliffs but they can climb to some extent, especially when a fallen tree is leaning at an acute angle. Once, when canoeing, I startled a beaver sitting on the trunk of a birch that had partly fallen into the water. The splash from the animal's belly flop was as unforgettable as seeing the rodent perched relatively high above the water's surface!

Not all food requires a danger-filled excursion onto land because ponds, especially long-established ones, contain a wealth of edible material. It is a common sight in late evening to see beavers floating on the water's surface, contentedly munching the leaves, stems, and flowers of water-lilies, water-shield, and other aquatic plants. Beavers also relish the submerged rhizomes of these plants, particularly yellow pond-lily, and chewed sections of those structures often adorn favourite dining sites. The high sodium content of these plants ensures that beavers do not run into a deficit of that important element.

A beaver's choice of food is seldom random. Food is carefully selected, largely by smell. With its enhanced olfactory capabilities a beaver is able to decipher not only the type of plant by its odour but also its palatability. Even when dining in the water, beavers periodically stop to smell their food, seemingly needing to confirm that what they are eating is actually edible.

For her Honours project, Esme Batten, a student of mine at Carleton University, tested a beaver's ability to select food by smell. By disguising inedible items with the scent of aspen, she found that beavers were fooled

into selecting those items and, by disguising aspen with the scent of inedible items, she made beavers ignore their favourite food!

One late November day years ago, I conducted a very crude test for a beaver's ability to discriminate by smell. It was overcast and the adult pair was busily working on a stand of poplars in the daytime, travelling up and down the same drag trail. When they were out of sight, I pulled across the trail a wind-felled trembling aspen that had been lying on the ground for a couple of years. Whenever the beavers encountered the tree, they would sniff it and then walk around it. When both beavers were out of sight in the pond, I pulled the tree off the trail and replaced it with a substantial aspen that they had cut down the previous night (I was much younger and

(Left) In early spring, the new growth of cattails and aquatic sedges is grazed.

(Below) Beavers sometimes graze on land, especially in early spring. Escape or "plunge" holes situated along the bank allow foragers to reach the safety of water more quickly.

stronger then!). When this roadblock was encountered, after sniffing the tree the beavers immediately began cutting through it. They worked on this tree for much of the day, removing branches and cutting the trunk into sections before dragging them down to the pond.

There is a small footnote to this story. When I first went to get a fresh-cut poplar, thinking both beavers were in the pond, I walked up their drag trail, straddling it with my feet so that I would not taint it with my scent. But one beaver was not in the pond, for it suddenly appeared on the trail, dragging a branch toward me. I froze so as not to frighten it. The beaver did not see me and kept coming closer. Finally, when only a couple of feet from me, it caught my scent. It dropped its branch, stood up on its hind legs, and began to growl. I suspect beads of sweat appeared on my forehead because the beaver's

(Right) Food is often eaten on favoured feeding "beds" that soon become littered with previously enjoyed meals.

(Below) Beavers select food primarily by smell.

(Right) This floating log is apparently ideal for dining on yellow pond-lily rhizomes.

(Opposite) Although conifers offer very little nutritional value, this feeding bed was littered with freshly debarked black spruce branches. Obviously the beaver had little else to eat.

head was just below waist level. After an agonizing minute, it dropped back down, grabbed the branch in its mouth, and resumed its journey to the pond, passing right between my legs in the process.

Without its chisel teeth a beaver cannot eat and would die from starvation. While too little tooth can be bad for a beaver, too much can also be fatal. There are records of beavers whose teeth did not properly wear and kept on growing until they eventually curled back into the skull, causing their owner to starve. Fortunately for beavers, this is apparently quite rare. For most beavers, their marvellous tree-felling tools come equipped with a lifetime warranty.

While essential for eating, the distinctive incisors of a beaver perform a much grander role. They bestow upon their owners the power to dramatically transform the landscape, a capability possessed by no other creature on this planet, apart from our species. Even then, beavers are unique, for when they alter the landscape innumerable plants and animals benefit.

Sadly, our species cannot make that same claim.

A beaver's teeth empower it with much more than just an ability to chew through wood.

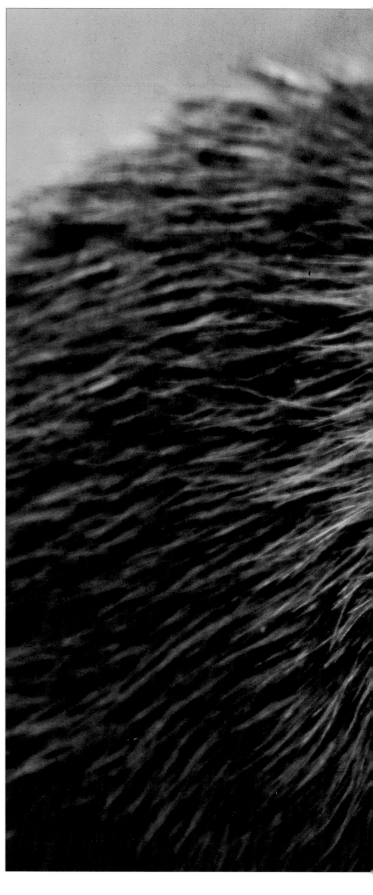

CHAPTER 4

DAM BUILDER

A beaver's life can be broken down into four main activities: sleeping, eating, grooming, and building and maintaining structures. Of course, there are other activities, such as scent marking and mating, but those four dominate much of a beaver's life, and are likely listed in the correct order if ranked by the amount of time an average beaver invests in each on a yearly basis. Because we usually cannot see what beavers do inside a lodge or under the water, we are biased in our observations and often think of beavers as investing an inordinate amount of time and effort into creating just three structures—dams, lodges, and winter food caches. Canals that are created to facilitate easier dragging of branches from land to the water might be thought of as a fourth type of structure, but these are dug and not constructed from materials. Regardless, all these activities have given rise to the belief that beavers are enterprising creatures, ones that we would do well to emulate. Perhaps we do just that, for not all beavers work equally hard, and many spend much of their time sleeping, eating, and fussing over their hair!

Of all of the structures made by beavers, the dam is their trademark. A dam is a wall of sticks, mud, and sometimes stones that on occasion reaches colossal

proportions and creates ponds large enough to be deemed small lakes. The current world record for length is a dam located in Alberta's Wood Buffalo National Park. Spanning 850 metres (2,788 feet), it was discovered by ecologist Jean Thie while looking at Google Earth images for beaver dams. Although long, the dam is not tall, with most of the structure being less than a metre (three feet) tall; table-flat, waterlogged boreal lowland creeks do not require much blockage to form big ponds. The record for height resides in Wyoming, where a dam reportedly stood 5.5 metres (18 feet) tall. Naturally, the vast majority

Beavers are unique among wild animals for their dam-building prowess.

The first stage of dam building is the placement of a row of limbs across the waterway. Note how the near end of the dam is anchored to the shore and the cut ends of the branches point downstream. River dams rarely survive the force of surging spring water.

construct dams. The pond that develops behind the dam provides safety and access to food. Beavers are extremely vulnerable on land and the farther into the forest they range in search of food, the more easily they fall prey to their main predators—gray wolves, eastern wolves (*C. lycaon*—a relatively new taxon), coyotes, and black bears. For a beaver, being near water means better odds of staying alive.

By obstructing the flow of water, a dam transforms a meandering stream into an ample pond, one that expands the contact zone between forest and water. As a pond grows, the number of trees that are safely accessible for beavers within a short distance of the water increases. The branches of trees and shrubs acquired on land are dragged back to the pond to be eaten in safety or stored for future use. Because branches can be pulled through the water with considerably less effort than when dragged on land, a pond also helps beavers conserve energy.

A pond provides another extremely important benefit. Even in the most northerly and coldest parts of their range, beavers do not hibernate. Active animals need a source of food, and during the winter a beaver's lifeline is usually a cache of branches stashed near the lodge. If the water freezes to the bottom of the pond, this cache becomes unavailable and the beavers, trapped inside their lodge, would starve. A dam, then, creates a water reservoir deep enough to stay unfrozen near the bottom, thereby ensuring the existence of an under-the-ice beaver thoroughfare for the duration of the long winter.

of dams throughout North America are considerably more modest in scale, averaging less than 50 metres (164 feet) long and two metres (6.5 feet) tall. Eurasian beavers also build dams but most seem to not reach the impressive stature of those erected by their North American counterparts.

It is the need for water that compels beavers to

But there is not always a need for beavers to build a dam. Lakes and other large bodies of water hold

substantial amounts of water and do not require a dam. If beavers do build one, it is often a rudimentary structure laid across a small outlet. Only when beavers colonize narrow and shallow bodies of water is a more substantial dam truly necessary.

Dams are often built across natural constrictions in waterways. While a logical site might be chosen for the dam's location, beavers are really not the master engineers that they are often reputed to be. Mistakes are sometimes made and dams placed across rivers in the fall seldom survive the spring surge of water.

Regardless of location, size, or shape, a dam is inevitably fabricated of sticks, vegetation, mud, and, where available, stones. In the first stage of dam building, branches are secured to the shore with mud, stones, and branches. From this rudimentary anchored base, the dam

Beavers use their mouth and dexterous front hands to position branches on a dam.

is gradually extended across the water, always with the cut end of the branches pointing downstream. With the crowns facing the current, the rudimentary dam serves to better catch and hold additional material. More branches are added until the framework is solid enough to hold mud and stones. Sticks and mud continue to be added from the upstream side of the dam, the current helping to keep them in place. Frequently, sticks that have had their bark eaten are added to the dam; beavers recycled materials long before that behaviour became fashionable in our species! Material is usually added to the downstream face of the dam by being pulled across from the upstream side.

Beavers transport construction materials in two different ways. They grab branches with their mouth, always near the cut end, and drag them over land and across water with the aid of powerful neck and jaw muscles. Mud and stones are cradled against their chest and under their chin with their front paws and forearms, carried in much the same way we transport a load of firewood. Beavers frequently transport mud and sticks

Because they grow next to water and are easy to cut and tow, alders are commonly used as building materials.

at the same time, a double carry that is most often performed in the context of lodge construction and maintenance. When doing a double carry, a beaver waddles on his hind two feet—a rather remarkable achievement for an animal that usually walks on all four limbs.

As a dam takes shape, the water on the upstream side starts to rise at a quickened pace when the constant application of mud begins to seal the spaces between the sticks. The water also adds material to the rudimentary dam as its current becomes impeded. As the dam develops and the incoming current slows even more, finer and lighter material helps seal smaller leaks. The build-up of material deposited on the upstream side of the dam gives it strength and stability, particularly with the weight of the water pushing against it. As long as water flows freely through or over the dam, beavers continue to add material, with spurts of activity occurring in spring following snowmelt, and in other seasons after heavy rains send an influx of water into the pond.

It was once believed that beavers swim along dams, visually searching for leaks. Beavers certainly make repairs whenever necessary, but how they determine when to go into action appears to involve little calculation on their part. In a novel study that involved audio recordings of rushing water and bathtubs, it was demonstrated that the sound of running water is an auditory stimulus that triggers dam-building behaviour. Thus, it seems that it is the sound of water rushing through a leak and not the intelligent analysis of structural integrity that inspires beavers to go into repair mode. Beavers can also detect a change in water speed and level, so these two stimuli also inspire a response in beavers.

A dam has a profound effect on the surrounding

A dam soon starts to back up water, turning a stream into a wider stream, and frequently a pond.

landscape. It holds back the water, causing it to rise and flood the adjacent forest floor. Trees with submerged roots slowly begin to drown. The incoming water, now slowed to a crawl, releases its organic cargo and this drifts slowly and steadily to the bottom. The newly drowned soil and vegetation also surrender their stores of nutrients to the water. The beavers take an active role in the enrichment process by dragging branches and leaves into the new pond and defecating in the water. In addition to being important reservoirs of water—ones that play essential roles in maintaining water tables, especially during drought—a beaver pond is a rich storehouse of minerals and organic compounds, a feature that ecologists call a "nutrient sink." Carbon is one element retained by beaver ponds and, like other elements, it goes through cycles, becoming transformed into different forms in the process. It remains locked in the pond sediments for a much longer period than it would in the former stream, taking more than 160 years (compared to 24 years in a

Beavers add material to dams from the upstream side.

(Above) When available, stones form part of the construction materials. These beavers appear to have been particularly industrious.

(Opposite) A beaver dam does more than add great beauty to the landscape. It can serve as a bridge for animals such as this white-tailed deer.

stream) for its "turnover" to be complete.

At certain times of the year, nutrients get flushed downstream from the pond, making it a "nutrient source" for other habitats. This feature is of particular importance in regions that are relatively nutrient deficient, including much of the vast boreal forest.

The sole purpose of a dam is to block the flow of water; beavers live in separate structures known as lodges—that are usually built at some distance from the dam. For many beavers, the lodge is a castle, complete with a moat that removes its occupants from virtually all danger. Even if a predator were to access a lodge, few have the physical strength to tear one open with the notable exception of bears. And even if the lodge's integrity were to be challenged, beavers could easily escape through one of their underwater entrances.

It has often been suggested that river otters are the beaver's main predator and that they enter lodges and even break dams in order to capture beavers. However, extensive research done on both species refutes these myths. Beavers and otters often co-inhabit the same ponds with no malice shown between them, and once, when canoeing, I came across a family of otters living in an abandoned beaver lodge while a family of beavers occupied another lodge close by. On one occasion, however, I did observe and videotape an aggressive interaction between those two species. It was shortly after dawn in mid-May, near the beaver birthing time, and three otters had climbed atop a beaver's feeding bed. From across the pond an adult beaver (likely the male) swam silently toward them. Just before it reached the otters, it dove and then a moment later launched itself onto the platform and, with teeth exposed, lunged at the otters. The startled creatures noisily snorted and chirped as they fell back frantically, finally jumping into the water. They swam out to the centre of the pond with the beaver in slow but determined pursuit. The beaver dove, vanished for a short time, and then suddenly emerged amongst the otters, slapping its tail as it surfaced. The visibly upset otters made a quick retreat to shore, hissing and snorting and looking over their shoulders as they nervously bounded out of sight.

Just as there is variance in the size and structure of dams, lodges differ in appearances and locations. Many are surrounded by water but some are built along the shore. Occasionally, natural cavities, such as rock caverns or hollows between tree roots, are incorporated into the structure of the lodge. Beavers sometimes excavate lodges in mud banks, adorning the entrance and bank

Image 1 and 2 shown

DAM BUILDER

109 shown

109

with a loose tangle of branches and an application of mud. In Europe, these "bank beavers" typically add only a sparse number of sticks and forgo the mud. Bank dens are sometimes used for short periods by dispersing beavers or males awaiting the birth of a new generation. Older ponds can have half a dozen lodges, with only a few active at a time. Sometimes a male will use one of the vacant structures as a "bachelor pad" while his mate gives birth and cares for the young in the main lodge. It has been reported that some colonies maintain two lodges, using one in summer and the other in winter. I once observed a colony switch from a summer lodge in one pond to a winter lodge in another pond on the other side of a narrow road. The switch may have been due to low water level in the summer pond. Humans had broken the dam in early spring, and an ensuing drought resulted in precariously low water levels, perhaps too low for beavers to remain in that pond for the winter.

A dam's magnitude cannot be properly ascertained from the pond side; only from the downstream side is the magnificence of the structure fully apparent.

With the exception of stones, the same types of materials that are used in the building of dams are

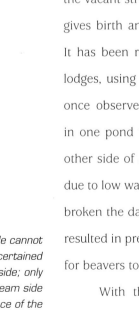

usually employed in the construction of lodges. When a lodge is built in the water, the first efforts involve piling up sticks and mud to create a firm platform that rises above the surface. Initially, fine branches, then coarser materials are piled on this base until a dome is created. Starting from near the bottom of the pond, at least one and often two or even more tunnels are dug and gnawed into the interior of the mound, which is further opened into a large chamber. While some animals eat themselves out of house and home, I suppose you might think of beavers as eating themselves *into* their home!

As a lodge nears its final form, mud is plastered over the outer surface. In northern regions, copious amounts of this material are added in the autumn to serve as insulation to keep out winter's chill. In spring, another coating of mud is sometimes added to replace that washed off by spring rains and snowmelt. In any season a fresh coat of mud makes recognition of an active lodge an easy feat.

To allow for air movement, the apex of the dome is reported to contain less mud than the rest of the lodge. Here, the air spaces in the tangle of branches form a

When water levels drop in a pond, the remarkable amount of mud and silt that accumulated on the upstream (pond) side of the dam is revealed. This material not only stops leaks but also strengthens the structure when the weight of the water pushes against it.

"chimney" that ensures a constant exchange of air between the exterior and interior of the lodge. Whether less mud is added deliberately or because this part of the lodge is more difficult to access when a beaver delivers a load of materials is an open question. Heat does rise, so it makes sense that inside the lodge, the upper centre of the roof would collect the greatest amount of heat, which would percolate through the sticks and melt the overlying snow. Thus, "chimney" is not really an accurate description of the lodge's air ventilation system, for there is no gaping hole leading into the lodge.

When watching a beaver add material to the top of his lodge, I observed a behaviour that planted a thought concerning the ventilation issue. It was late July and a beaver had been busy depositing mud and sticks on top of the lodge. In a three-hour period, it made 10 trips, always using the "double-carry" (sticks held in its mouth, mud pressed against its chin and upper chest). Usually it would climb up and drop its load of mud, then make some effort to position the sticks. But on two occasions it did something quite different. On those trips it carried, in addition to a load of mud, a relatively

Beavers swim by their dams on a regular basis, attracted to leaks by the sound and movement of escaping water.

straight trembling aspen branch (identified by its smooth pale green bark) that was a bit more than a metre (three feet) long. These were treated differently than any other stick carried atop the lodge. After it dropped its mud load, the beaver held these sticks vertically in the air and shoved them down into the top of the lodge. Once the stick penetrated the surface of the lodge, it was gradually pushed down with force until its top end was flush with the top of the lodge. Due to the length of the sticks, I wondered if they had not gone right through the roof and were protruding inside the lodge. If so, it would be a novel way to deliver edible material to the kits that I could hear noisily mewing inside the lodge. If the portion of the stick protruding inside was eaten, the rest would remain embedded in the lodge's roof. Was the beaver solving two problems with one novel solution? And if the sticks were pulled completely through the roof from inside the lodge, would the resulting puncture

(Above) When a leak is found, mud, when available, is dredged up from the bottom on the upstream side and shoved into place. Plants and woody materials are soon added, sometimes "borrowed" from other parts of the dam.

(Right) After a sojourn downstream, a beaver returns to its pond on the other side of the dam.

(Above) On older dams, material is added to the downstream side by being pulled across the top of the structure.

(Opposite top) While large logs are usually not added to dams during early construction stages, they are often found on long-established dams.

(Opposite bottom) Stretching half a mile, this dam in Wood Buffalo National Park in Alberta is the longest in the world. The lodge lies in the open water just above the outflowing creek, which is dammed, of course. (Photo © Parks Canada)

holes not then provide ventilation? Obviously it is impossible to draw any conclusions from a mere couple of observations, especially when closer examination had not been conducted and the true fate of the sticks never determined. Indeed, it could well be that the sticks were simply being shoved into the roof to strengthen it and never did actually protrude into the lodge.

Ventilation is especially important in winter because during that season beavers spend more time inside their lodge than they do at any other time of the year. And several generations share the space for many months. The lodge's interior chamber usually contains a couple of levels, with the highest one serving as the

sleeping quarters. This level is carpeted with strips of bark, which are regularly replaced. The lower portion, the one nearest the main entrance, serves as the dining room.

Before a lodge is constructed, dispersing beavers need a temporary residence. Sometimes a previously occupied lodge is used. Occasionally these are treated as "fixer-uppers" and get refurbished, sparing the beavers the effort of starting a new lodge from scratch. Newly formed ponds or narrow waterways being traversed rarely possess abandoned lodges, so a beaver must find somewhere else to hang its hat until a new home is built. On those occasions, beavers will sleep on the shore or

in a natural or beaver-made den. In one new pond, I observed a beaver sleeping on a beautiful moss-covered rock ledge at the water's edge. In another, a beaver slept atop the lodge it was constructing. Until the new lodge is ready for occupancy, beavers that sleep out in the open are at considerable risk.

The beavers that create new ponds and lodges are most often two-year-olds dispersing from the family pond. Long-established ponds usually support a colony of six to eight beavers, consisting of an adult pair, their previous year's young (one-year-olds), and anywhere

from two to four new beaver kits. If food is quite plentiful, the two-year-olds sometimes remain with the colony for another year, bringing the colony membership towards a dozen. Usually the two-year-olds depart around the time their newest siblings are born. Dispersing youngsters seem lonely and are more than willing to latch on to another beaver. By imitating its soft whines, on a couple of occasions I enticed what I suspected to be a dispersing beaver to my canoe and had it follow me for some distance. Whether the adults drive the adolescent beavers out of the colony or if they leave of their own accord is not clear, but

Some ponds lie behind a series of dams, each of which helps maintain the water level in the pond.

it may well be that, more often than not, they are strongly encouraged to go their own way.

Between late April and mid-May, I have on several occasions observed aggressive behaviour between adults and their oldest offspring. Twice I observed a presumed two-year-old and an adult pressing their faces against one another while in the water (with the two possibly locking teeth), and then pushing against each other, spinning around in a circular "dance" on the pond's surface. Perhaps this was a demonstration of dominance and strength? After the "dance" was over, the larger beaver appeared to reject the smaller one's advances. Once I also watched an adult (the male?) display aggression toward a young beaver (again, presumably a two-year-old). After first driving it away, it snuck up on the youngster while it groomed itself atop a floating bog mat. When near enough, the adult lunged and appeared to grab the groomer's tail in its mouth (vegetation on the bog mat unfortunately prevented an unobstructed view). Only after a frantic attempt at a couple of leaps was the panic-stricken youngster able to pull free and escape. This interaction took place in mid-May, just around the

Dams create reservoirs of water essential for maintaining local water tables, especially in times of drought.

(Right and opposite) High water levels in early spring and autumn provide a flush of oxygen into the pond, and a flush of nutrients out of it.

time baby beavers are born. Many beavers sport nicks on their tails, so perhaps this form of aggressive behaviour between adults and their young is not rare.

Most often, dispersing beavers head downstream —a direction that in studies is chosen almost twice as frequently as an upstream direction. Initially, short return trips may be made, perhaps to develop familiarity with foreign terrain. Dispersing juveniles are known to occasionally return to their natal colony and spend another winter with their family. The distance a young beaver ultimately disperses to depends on a number of factors, including the suitability of the new terrain and whether or not other beavers are already present in the first sites it arrives at.

Wandering beavers often encounter another of the opposite sex on their journeys and the pair travels together, eventually establishing a new colony in a suitable habitat. In other instances, a disperser shows up at a newly established lodge and pairs up with the homesteader. In either case, the days of loneliness eventually end for single beavers.

When an area is colonized, "No Trespassing"

notices soon get posted. These are mounds or exposed sites adorned with special chemicals that deliver an unmistakable message to a recipient's nose. The scents are produced in two pairs of internal structures located between the base of the tail and the pelvis. Castor sacs are pouches extending from the urinary tract. They store and release castoreum, which gets flushed through the cloaca when urine is diverted through the sacs. Castoreum is a complex substance—possibly containing as many as a hundred components—derived in part from plant defence chemicals known as "secondary metabolites," which are acquired in the beaver's diet. One of these compounds is salicylic acid, the medicinal ingredient of aspirin. This compound is sequestered from willows, which are an important food for beavers around the

(Above and left) Through time, old dams support floral gardens, and become transit ways for animals as large as moose.

A dam creates a pond, but a lodge houses the beavers.
(Right) Many a beaver's lodge is a castle surrounded by a very large moat!

A muskrat lodge can be easily told from a beaver's by the absence of sticks. Muskrats characteristically build their lodges from softer material such as cattail stalks.

world. *Nuphar* water-lilies, rich in alkaloid compounds, are thought to be important for the production of the castoreum component castoramine. Beavers are an excellent example of how animals have evolved ways to harmlessly ingest and then exploit for their own purposes the very chemicals that plants produce to keep herbivores at bay. While some (such as caterpillars with poison spines) store and use the chemicals for their own defence, beavers employ them as olfactory declarations of territory ownership. Both sexes produce castoreum but males post their pungent scents much more frequently than do females, especially in spring. Castoreum is usually released on raised sites called scent mounds, but it is believed that beavers also release castoreum directly into the water, thereby using it as an olfactory highway.

Anal glands are different than castor sacs in two ways. One is that the linings of their compartments secrete the glands' chemical compounds, which are oily—a feature that gave rise to the moniker "oil glands."

(Top) An abandoned lodge is examined as a possible fixer-upper. (Bottom) In late spring and early summer, new lodges are built by dispersing beavers.

(Above) It is remarkable that beavers in bipedal mode successfully carry heavy loads up steep slopes full of trip hazards without seeing their feet!

(Opposite) A lodge's entrances are not visible unless the water level drops. When it does, two entrances are usually revealed. The one on the right has a canal leading up to it.

Like castor sacs, the glands release their products through the cloaca, a body opening shared by the reproductive and digestive tracts. The other difference is that unlike the contents of the castor sacs that are flushed out by urine, anal gland secretions are released after physical stimulation of papillae, nipple-like projections that protrude through the cloaca when releasing anal gland secretions.

Castoreum is the primary chemical used as a territorial marker but both types of chemical products are released on top of scent mounds, which are usually piles of mud (sometimes small amounts of vegetation are used either in combination with the mud or on their own) placed atop rocks, logs, dams, or the shores around a beaver's territory. Materials on the mound are frequently pulled toward and under the beaver with its front paws. Eurasian beavers do not dredge up mud from the bottom of waterways like North American beavers do, hence their scent "mounds" are often not much more than an elevated muddy spot on a creek or river bank. The extra elevation helps disperse the odours over a wider area and the mud helps intensify the scent much in the way a wet dog's hairs release a lot more odour. Castoreum

is expelled when the beaver urinates from a hunched position over the mound but a beaver drags its cloaca across a mound when it is adorning it with anal gland secretions. It has been found that castoreum predominately performs the role of territory ownership declaration while anal gland secretions serve to provide a basis for individual identification.

Extensive scent marking occurs in spring, the time when two-year-old beavers are on the move and birthing is taking place. Scent mounds are most actively maintained in densely populated regions but reportedly are not always produced in isolated colonies, likely because there is less danger of encroachment by foreign beavers. They are often more densely situated upstream from the lodge, likely because dispersing beavers tend more often than not to move downstream. Extensive studies performed on scent marking in both North American and Eurasian beavers revealed that marking is reduced when predators are detected. A beaver out of the water is at risk and thus scent marking certainly has danger associated with it. Like other activities, such as foraging on land, there is a cost-benefit balance that must be considered.

Where do beavers sleep until a lodge is built? (Opposite) Some sleep atop an old lodge they are refurbishing, (above) occasionally sleeping on their backs! (Left) This beaver found an ideal temporary bed on a moss-covered rock ledge.

(Top) A colony usually consists of three ages of beavers: adults and two generations of offspring.

(Bottom and opposite) Baby beavers usually start venturing outside the lodge after a month or so. These kits are only a couple of months old.

Each beaver has its own chemical fingerprint (largely due to the secretions of the anal glands) and colony members readily recognize a stranger travelling through their real estate by its smell. Intruders that fail to heed the chemical warnings are physically repelled, suggesting that the nicks visible in the tails of many beavers are sometimes received during territorial encroachments. It has also been found that dispersing beavers recognize kin they had never previously met (such as colony members that dispersed in previous years). This ability to recognize close relatives reduces the chances of choosing one as a mate, and thus acts as a safeguard against inbreeding.

A remarkable display of territory advertisement known as the "stick display" has been observed being performed by Eurasian beavers. In this display, a beaver rises up from shallow water with a stick held in its mouth and forepaws. The animal bobs its upper body up and down, with the stick sometimes splashing in the water. This display was observed occurring at territory boundaries, with the beaver in the adjoining territory sometimes responding with its own stick display. Scent marking usually preceded the display, which occasionally

took place on land where no splashing was produced, leading to the conclusion that this territorial warning is intended to be more visual than audible.

Scent marking occurs with a vengeance after a territorial intrusion. I once came across two beavers fighting in Basin Creek, a narrow stream that flows from Basin Lake into the Bonnechere River in Algonquin Provincial Park. I was walking across the small bridge that fords the creek when I heard loud splashing on the upstream side. I looked to see the water boiling but could not discern what was thrashing about. A moment later, the commotion stopped and, to my surprise, a large beaver swam to shore. Seconds later it launched itself back into the water and went head to head with another beaver of equal size. Like Sumo wrestlers they grappled with their forearms, rolling and writhing around in and under the water as each strove to gain physical advantage over the other. They appeared to bite each other in the

upper body region but, with their constant motion, this was hard to discern. (Later I reviewed the photos and could see blood in the water, indicating at least one of the combatants had received a serious injury.) After a minute or so of violent fighting, they separated. The suspected loser, who appeared to have a gash across the right side of its face, retreated to the far shore where it floated motionless, keeping a very low profile in the water. The apparent victor and territory owner climbed up on the opposite bank and sat very still, breathing heavily from the physical exertion. Every few seconds it would utter a pitiful whine and its body periodically trembled. Its left forearm was held at a peculiar angle and it appeared that the beaver had been bitten on its left shoulder.

After about 15 minutes or so, the animal made a weak attempt to groom its face with its right front hand, but when it tried to do the same with its left it seemed unable to raise that arm. The beaver then squatted and released some scent before slowly waddling back into the water. It slowly swam upstream, going ashore twice to scent mark on what appeared to be scent mounds. As it neared the final site, it dove and then brought up a

(Opposite and above) The youngest members of the colony seldom stray far from their parents.

(Top) Some lodges are built along the edge of shoreline vegetation, while others (bottom) are located right on the shore, especially when beavers inhabit deep lakes.

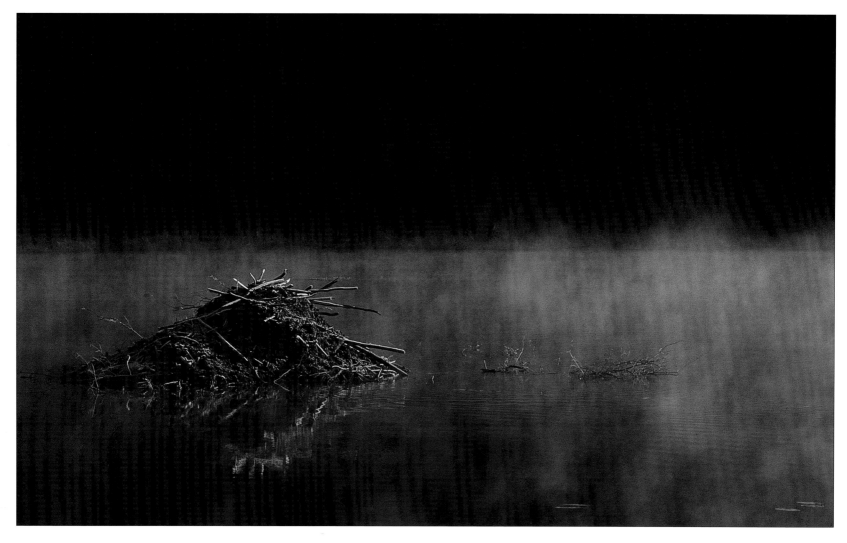

load of mud next to the shore. With its back to me, it slowly climbed up on land, but appeared to be having difficulty holding the material on its left side. The mud was dropped atop a previously established scent mound and over this the beaver squatted and released its scent. When the animal returned to the water it swam farther upstream, and I raced from the bridge through some alders to a small opening directly across the creek from this scent mound and plopped down, remaining motionless. A moment later I heard a tail slap, and a short time later the beaver reappeared, swimming downstream. As it passed by me, I could hear the animal either breathing heavily in short bursts or softly snorting. I think it was the former as it was undoubtedly still exhausted from the immense amount of energy it expended during the fight. The beaver slapped its tail twice more, including once where the fight had taken place, before turning back upstream. As it passed by me it dove, reappearing a few seconds later along the opposite shore where it climbed up, holding a fresh load of mud against its chest, again seeming to have difficulty holding with its left forearm. It dropped the mud on top of its recently scented mound and then squatted and deposited a fresh dose of castoreum before returning to the water and disappearing upstream. While territorial intrusions never end amicably, I suspect that serious fighting, such

Lodges built by North American beavers are typically surrounded by water.

as I observed, is seldom witnessed. Fighting in Eurasian beavers is reportedly more commonly observed, especially in the fall when beavers are ranging more widely to gather food for storage. Howard Parker at Telemark University College has found that hides of Eurasian beavers regularly contain nick marks inflicted by the teeth of other beavers. But as many North American beavers, especially adult males, sport nicks in their tails, aggressive interactions in that species may also occur relatively frequently.

If one member of a resident pair of beavers dies, the other will re-mate. Beavers were thought to be strictly monogamous animals that paired for life but in Illinois, DNA studies revealed that while beavers may appear to be faithfully monogamous and some no doubt are, females occasionally give birth to young sired by a neighbouring male. It seems that in many species of animals, "monogamous" females are willing to enrich the gene pool of their offspring if given the chance. And male animals usually seem more than willing to help

(Above) Occasionally beavers attach a second lodge to the first, thus creating a semi-detached!

(Right) Older ponds often contain more than one lodge. While some remain unused, others might house beavers on a part-time basis, sometimes during the birthing season.

them out whenever the opportunity arises. Of interest, in the Illinois study, kits born from extramarital unions sometimes moved back and forth between the different parents' colonies. As beavers recognize relatives through their anal gland secretions, it seems likely that the father would recognize his own young. It appears that his visiting rights were flexible, not fixed!

Many beavers breed in February but the time of year varies with location, with mating occurring later in the north. Copulation is reported to occur underwater. After a gestation period of about three months, three to four kits are born inside the lodge. Newborns are rarely seen outside the lodge until their first month has passed and they are weaned off the mother's milk. The young are born quite precocial (active, fully furred, eyes open or opening within hours after birth), and are able to eat solid foods after a couple of weeks. They can swim after only days, but apparently the fur of a newborn is not waterproof. As a kit's anal glands do not function until it is three to four weeks old, and its fur is reported not to be waterproof until the youngster is almost two months of age, there is once again circumstantial evidence

(Above) A behaviour unknown in their Eurasian relatives, North American beavers sometimes create "giant" scent mounds.

(Opposite) Beavers mark their territories with scent mounds—raised areas onto which castoreum is released. North American beavers typically carry mud onto the site before scent marking. Anal gland secretions are also released on the mound but these require physical stimulation of the cloaca, as this beaver is doing.

142

that anal gland secretions have a waterproofing role in North American beavers. A young beaver spends its first year in relative leisure but eventually starts taking part in the colony's activities. In its second year it becomes more involved in colonial duties, including caring for its younger siblings.

Some colonies are active in the same pond for decades; others exist for a much shorter period of time. Ponds created in relatively foodless habitats (often by dispersers) may be abandoned if the beaver or beavers are fortunate enough to survive their first winter. Food supply appears to be the main factor that determines a colony's longevity; beavers vanish from ponds around which most of the edible food has been extracted. A lack of water can also stimulate abandonment, and, of course, if the resident beavers are killed, the colony and eventually the pond exist no more. It has been suggested that the average lifespan of a colony pond is about 10 years.

An active beaver lodge usually houses more than just beavers. Several species of small "beaver beetles"

(Opposite) More aggressive interactions occur between adults during territorial intrusions. After colliding head to head, these two fought violently for several minutes, wrestling and biting each other, with one eventually receiving a serious shoulder wound.

(Above) For nearly half an hour the injured victor sat on shore, favouring its left forearm, repeatedly trembling and whining.

After it returned to the water, the injured victor began to scent mark along the shore. (Top left) Here it deposits fresh mud atop a scent mound, having difficulty using its left forearm. (Top right) Next it releases castoreum on the mound; if you look closely you can see the urine streaming behind its right hind leg.

(Right) Beavers often sport nicks on their tails, most likely acquired during territorial disputes.

live inside a lodge or under the fur of a living beaver. The beaver's "guests" are flattened so that they can slip through the dense pelt. Trappers sometimes think they caught a flea-ridden beaver when little insects start leaving the corpse en masse. However, beaver beetles do not damage the animal's hide, for they feed on dead skin and other detritus, not the beaver's blood. They are leaving the beaver only because their meal ticket has gone cold.

On occasion, muskrats and, reportedly, voles have been found co-inhabiting active lodges. I have not only observed muskrats swimming in and out of beaver-occupied lodges with impunity but also eating the bark from branches in food piles that were created by the beavers for winter consumption.

Because of a dependency on water, beavers create ponds. In addition to serving the needs of their makers,

A behaviour not known to occur in North American beavers, the stick display has been observed in territorial Eurasian beavers in Norway. (Photo credit: Orsolya Haarberg/Samfoto/ The Canadian Press)

the ponds play other, equally important roles. They are extremely important in maintaining water tables, especially in times of drought. The water impounded by a beaver dam seeps into the soil, replenishing and stabilizing underground reserves that can extend, depending on the lay of the land, as far as a couple of kilometres from the pond. When drought parches the land, a water table supported by a beaver pond might fall only a few centimetres (an inch or so), while in sites distant to the pond's influence, the drop can be more than a metre (three feet).

In addition to their hydrological functions, beaver ponds play extremely important ecological roles. The reservoir of stilled water, the seeping dam, the muddy shores, the drowned trees—every facet of a beaver pond provides opportunities for countless plants and animals. By modifying the landscape to suit their own needs, beavers create oases of life. For this they have deservedly been awarded the titles "ecosystem engineers" and "keystone species."

In an unusual spring behaviour that I call "the dance," an adult and presumably a two-year-old press their faces together and push hard, ending up rotating in a circle on the pond's surface. At times it appears their teeth are locked together.

CHAPTER 5

OASIS OF LIFE

Waiting quietly by a beaver pond just as the dawn breaks is like sitting in the grandest of theatres awaiting with eager anticipation the start of a great play. In the dim light, you are keenly aware of subtle sounds and nearly discernible movements of players on the stage, but you resist the temptation to put unearthly forms to their sources. Then, as if heavy velvet curtains were being lifted one by one, or if stage lights were slowly being raised, the darkness begins to dissolve into light. As the darkness fades, you are soon immersed in a world of increasing motion and sound. Ponderous wings part the mist as a great blue heron arrives at the pond. A rubbery squeak followed by a splash foretells a territorial dispute being settled by a green frog. Undulating movement along the dam catches your eye and you look to see a mink patrolling for its breakfast, perhaps the frog that had just squealed. With soft twitters, a pair of tree swallows perched atop a dead tree serenade the return of food-bringing light. Nearby, bubbles break the water's stillness. They turn into ripples that grow and swell into a massive head. You move to get a better view and instantly the water explodes as the beaver that emerged for one last mission tells you in plain beaver language what it thinks of your intrusion. Heart pounding, you return to

your motionless vigil. After swimming a dozen laps and slapping its tail half that number of times, the beaver ascertains that all is well and climbs atop a well-trampled platform on a peat island. It turns toward the warming light and sits upright, its paddle tail projecting forward between its legs, and begins to groom its plush coat of fur. When its lengthy ablution is finally complete, the beaver slips back into the water. A short swim and then, with silent deliberation, it slides beneath the surface and vanishes for the day. The sun now peers over the trees and its warming gaze banishes the last of the mist spirits

(Above) A beaver pond provides habitat for myriad plants and animals.

(Opposite) While this female mallard and her young sitting on a beaver dam have nothing to fear from the bull moose, there are real dangers to be on the watch for.

from the pond. Its warmth removes the chill from your bones and penetrates your soul. You feel exhilarated, even slightly intoxicated, for you have experienced not just the breaking of the day but the essence of life itself. You leave, knowing that when you return another day, the pond will offer a different production, with new players joining familiar favourites, with roles and plots changing under the attentive direction of time.

Beaver ponds are home to many plants and animals whose abundance and diversity changes as the pond ages. A new pond initially supports a meagre assemblage of organisms but as it matures, the bottom sediments thicken and they and the water become enriched with nutrients. Some, such as calcium, are present in a form readily used by plants. Others, such as phosphorus,

The large floating leaves of white water-lilies (bottom) and yellow pond-lilies (top) soon make an appearance in established ponds.

require the work of bacteria to transform them into a plant-friendly form. Those single-celled organisms thrive in the warm muck where they extract what they need from the organic debris. Shunning the aid of oxygen, anaerobic bacteria transform compounds into even smaller components, many of which remain locked in the bottom until it is disturbed by the actions of winds or large creatures. When oxygen infiltrates the muck, aerobic bacteria—bacteria that cannot function in its absence—complete the task of turning tissues into their basic components. When ponds swell with snowmelt or deluges of rain, nutrients are liberated from the bottom and swept over the dam and out of the pond. Beaver ponds provide a supply of otherwise scarce nutrients to waters downstream of the dam, a feature of special importance in northern, nutrient-poor regions.

Nitrogen is another element essential for life, but it often occurs in a gaseous form that plants cannot use. However, when converted to a plant-friendly form such as nitrate, plants quickly incorporate it into their growth. An excess of nitrate in an aquatic system leads to an explosion of algal growth, which in turn leads to

Water pH and temperature, and nearness to a source of seeds are factors that determine what plants grow in a pond. Water smartweed is found in those that retain a bit of current.

eutrophication—a lack of oxygen due to its consumption by microbes that decompose dead plants. Beaver ponds can reduce the flow of nitrates through a stream system by locking them up in the bottom sediments where they become converted into gaseous nitrogen, which plants cannot utilize. This process can be a very important function in landscapes where streams flow through heavily fertilized agricultural land. In this setting, beaver ponds behave like living filters.

The pond's rich array of organic compounds supports a variety of plants whose seeds arrive in a number of ways. Those of water-lilies often float on the stream that feeds the pond. Swamp milkweed seeds drift in on silk parachutes powered by the wind. Jewelweeds leap frog around the pond's perimeter, growing from seeds ejected from the mother plant's volatile seedpods. The seeds of beggar's-ticks hitch rides on moose and other animals travelling from pond to pond. The feathers and feet of ducks and herons can transport not only seeds but also entire plants; small colonies of duckweeds arrive courtesy of these aerial taxicabs.

In only a matter of years, a pond begins to support an array of plants much higher in diversity than found along the undammed stream. Studies have found that up to 25 percent of the plants growing around the edge of a beaver pond—the riparian zone—may primarily be there courtesy of beavers.

Through time, several distinct zones of plant life become established. Along the shore grow plants that like to keep their feet damp, beauties such as orange jewelweed and swamp milkweed, which peer out from bouquets of sedges. Next to the shore the stunning blooms of blue flag emerge from the shallow water. From

(Left) Several distinct zones of plants eventually develop in a pond, with some such as the tussock-forming woolgrass (which is not a grass but a sedge) growing near the shore in the emergent zone where the plants' leaves and flowers are all above water.

(Opposite) It is obvious that yellow water-crowfoots, which grow in the floating-leaf zone (where the plants' stems are submerged but their leaves and flowers float on the surface), found the conditions in this pond to be to their liking.

(Above) Water-shield is often one of the most common floating-leaved aquatics found in beaver ponds.

(Opposite right) All plants are food for some animal and water-shield is no exception, as this water-lily leaf beetle reveals.

(Opposite left) A few Lepidoptera, such as the caterpillars of this aquatic snout moth, also take advantage of the floating bounty.

this zone extending into and sometimes right across the pond are the plants whose rhizomes grip the bottom while their leaves and flowers float on the surface. The submerged stems of water-lilies form jungle-like tangles in which skimmer dragonfly nymphs sit waiting with lethal patience for meals to swim by. High above, the floating leaves provide perches for bullfrogs and vesper bluets, yellow damselflies that make an appearance only after the sun has slipped out of sight. Among the large leaves free-float the tiny leaves of duckweed and the even more diminutive leaves of wolffia, the smallest flowering plant in the world.

By mid-summer the leaves of aquatic plants reveal their importance as food for small animals. Rare are those not riddled with holes and channels chewed by beetles and their grubs; the larvae of leaf-mining flies and aquatic snout moths embed their own gastronomically-inspired artwork in the floating leaves. The aquatic plants also fuel the needs of much larger animals. Moose gorge on water-shield for hours at a time, gleaning precious sodium from the floating leaves and stems. Beaver ponds supply many of these giants with their main supply of this mineral, which is stored in the rumen for use later in the year; if it were not for beavers, there would most likely be fewer

of these majestic beasts in northern regions. Even porcupines visit the edges of beaver ponds on occasion for a sodium fix. The aquatic plants also hold great appeal for beavers, which devour all parts, displaying a particular fondness for the submerged rhizomes, especially of yellow pond-lilies. When pieces of a rhizome break off and sink to the bottom, they can sprout new plants. Thus, in some ways, beavers act like aquatic farmers, albeit unintentional ones, sowing "seeds" for future harvest. Beavers derive another, quite unusual benefit from waterlilies. Some of the plant's defensive chemicals are sequestered and used to produce castoreum.

For every large animal that makes its way through a beaver pond, there are exponentially more small ones in residence. The density of pond-dwelling invertebrates is much higher than that which was found in the original pre-dam stream. In fact, it can be astronomical, reaching as high as 73,000 organisms per square metre! The bottom mud is alive with the maggots of midges, flies that as adults bear an uncanny similarity to mosquitoes, so

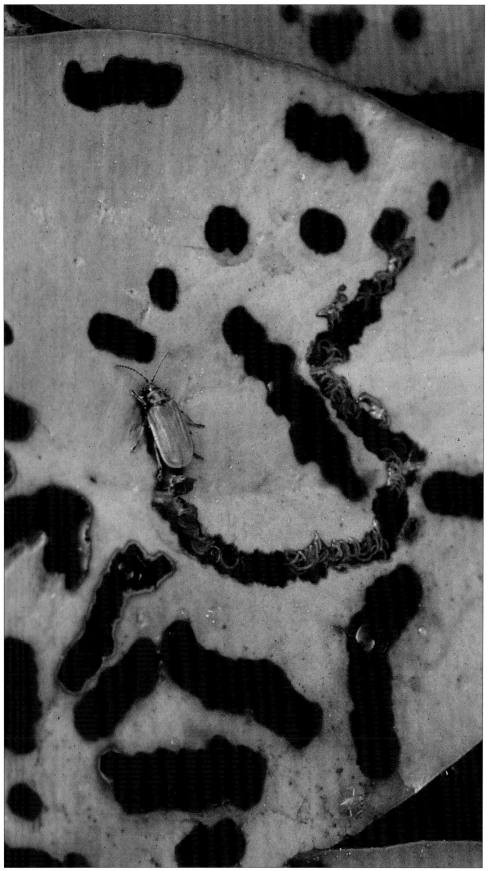

much so that their evening swarms strike terror into the uninformed. It may come as a surprise that beaver ponds are not ideal breeding grounds for mosquitoes. That is because they harbour numerous predators that would eagerly gobble up the wriggling larvae. Backswimmers, water boatmen, pygmy backswimmers, giant water bugs, diving beetles, predaceous diving beetles, water scorpions, and nymphs of dragonflies and damselflies—while not all of these predators dine on mosquito larvae, their diversity and numbers present a gauntlet through which many small creatures fail to pass unscathed.

(Above) Muskrats commonly co-inhabit beaver ponds, dining on the emergent vegetation.

(Right) The leaves of aquatic plants like water-shield contain four to five hundred times more sodium than many of the terrestrial plants growing around a pond, which is why moose spend so much time visiting beaver ponds in summer.

The midges and other insects emerging from beaver ponds can be up to five times more numerous than those arising from other bodies of water. This has great implications for the fauna that harvests these insects. Not only birds benefit; certain species of bats have been found to be more numerous foraging over beaver ponds than above similar-sized water bodies lacking beavers.

Every part of a beaver pond houses its own collection of creatures. Dams are home to black fly larvae

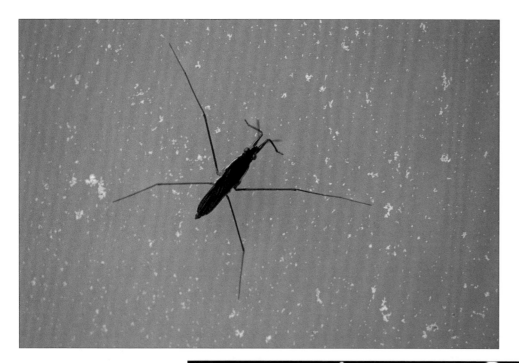

that use the submerged sticks as anchors while the flowing water brings them their food. Lodges house more than their makers. Several types of small beetles share the beaver's lodge, and on occasion, muskrats and even voles do, too. Vacant lodges can house families of river otters. The beavers themselves are habitat for *Platypsyllus castoris*, the beaver beetle, which spends most of its adult life roaming its host. These small, blind, flightless beetles live next to a beaver's skin, their flattened bodies enabling them to crawl through the base of the dense pelt as they devour the dead skin of their host. Even when a beaver swims underwater, the beetles do not drown, for

(Above) Predatory insects abound in beaver ponds. Water striders hunt on the surface, using vibration sensors in their legs and antennae to detect prey.

(Right) Whirligigs are predatory beetles whose large eyes simultaneously see below and above the water's surface. Special ear-like antennae detect vibrations, allowing these unusual animals to aggregate in large groups and swirl around without ever bumping into each other.

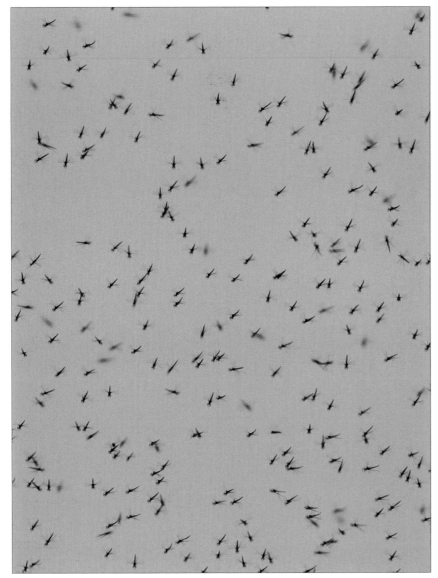

water never reaches the base of a beaver's fur coat.

While most of the plants in beaver ponds are food for animals, there are some that have reversed the traditional roles. Tiny yellow blooms sticking out of the water are innocuous flags marking the presence of one of the deadliest plants in the pond, deadly, that is, if you are a tiny insect or water flea. Suspended beneath the surface is the bladderwort's death net—a labyrinth of underwater stems that contain hundreds of little leaf traps—tiny bladder-like balls that implosively open when a hair trigger is touched. After sucking in the water surrounding the trap's tripwire, the bladder snaps shut, sentencing its prisoner to certain death. Other carnivorous plants frequent beaver ponds but they perform their executions out of the water and on the shore, or atop floating logs. Sundews sport small leaf pads that use glue-laden knobbed hairs to snag prey. Once an insect has been secured, the leaf pad slowly folds over, giving the hapless creature a lethal embrace as digestive enzymes are released from the shorter knobbed hairs more central in the pad.

The plethora of insects in a beaver pond is food

Mating swarms of midges reflect the abundance of their larvae that live in the muddy bottom of the pond. The flying adults are important food for insectivorous birds and predatory invertebrates, including spiders.

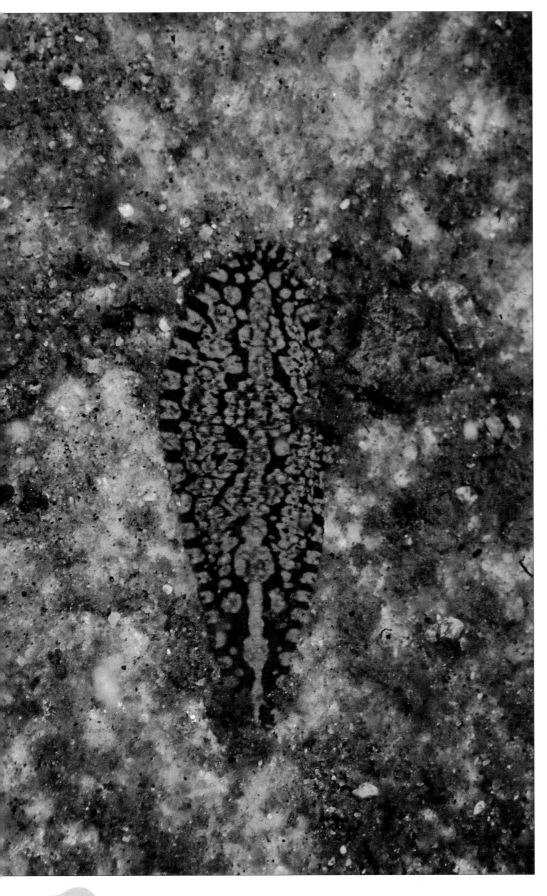

for animals both above and below the water. When the aquatic larve of caddisflies, mayflies, and midges emerge from the water and shed their larval prisons in favour of wings, they are besieged by frogs, adult dragonflies, swallows, kingbirds, waxwings, and fly-catching warblers. In northern ponds, Bonaparte's gulls join the aerial assault. During their brief migration from the water to transform from pond-dwelling nymphs to flying adults, dragonflies are ravaged by grackles and red-winged blackbirds. Beneath the water's surface the danger is no less. In addition to predatory insects, hooded mergansers and small fish continue the attack. Red-bellied dace, tiny fish that remain minnows for life, often gather near the beavers' lodge and food pile where their insect quarry tends to be more numerous. The dace, in turn, are food for larger fish and mink, which weave their way through the cache's tangle of branches. Bullheads, small relatives of catfish, comb the pond's bottom with their whiskers, seeking tasty morsels to eat. These slow-moving fish catch the eye of great blue herons standing motionless in the water, patiently waiting for a meal to swim into range of their lethal bills. Bullheads are also a favoured food of river otters, which in winter use the pond's frozen surface as a dining table. Those semi-aquatic weasels are intricately linked to beaver-inhabited waterways; studies have shown otters avoid watersheds that lack beaver dams. This is undoubtedly because beaver ponds harbour slow-swimming fish, which otters have an easy time catching, and are deep enough to allow these large weasels to fully utilize their underwater skills.

In addition to animals that exploit living creatures in the pond there are those that deal with the dead and dying. Painted, snapping, and other pond-dwelling

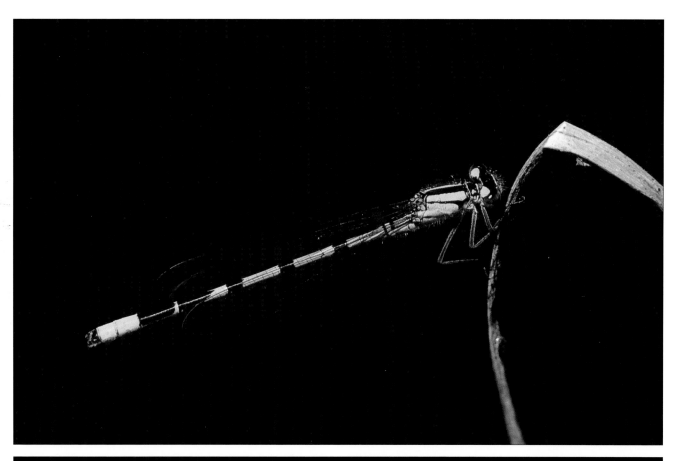

(Opposite) Many small animals live in the warm still water of beaver ponds. Placobdella parasitica *is a beautiful leech often found attached to snapping turtles.*

(Top) Beaver ponds provide habitat for the nymphs of numerous odonates. The adult stages of damselflies (here a boreal bluet) are commonly encountered around the pond edges.

(Bottom) Female sedge sprites lay their eggs in slightly submerged plant tissues while the males quite literally stand guard, attached by claspers to the back of the female's head.

(Top) The names of a couple of dragonflies reflect their penchant for laying their eggs in beaver ponds. Beaverpond baskettails are also named for the way the female's abdomen curls to form a basket when she lays eggs.

(Bottom right) A beaverpond clubtail (here a female) belongs to a group named after the pronounced flaring of the distal end of their abdomen. (Bottom left) While dragonfly nymphs are not easily seen underwater, after they emerge to transform into the adult flying form, their lifeless cases decorate plants and rocks all through the pond. Here a female white-faced meadowhawk escapes her nymphal prison.

turtles do kill living prey but also scavenge carcasses. Beaver ponds are extremely important habitat for many species, and studies have revealed, of no surprise, that the diversity and abundance of reptiles (including snakes) is higher in beaver-altered waterways. Turtles abound in older ponds, the leathery base of their legs often housing a complement of leeches. By basking on moss-covered logs, skeletons of the once-tall trees drowned by the pond, the turtles rid themselves of these and other undesired passengers, and raise their body temperature too. Not all leeches are parasitic; some are strictly scavengers and others exhibit a predatory lifestyle.

Beaver ponds are also important habitat for many

amphibians. Some, such as bullfrogs and mink frogs, can be found in the pond year-round. Depending on the species, for one to two years they live as swimming tadpoles, which are nothing less than eating machines owning intestines that comprise half of their body mass. Their diet is largely algae, which they graze from submerged plant debris and the bottom of floating leaves. The tail-less, legged adults spend winter in a death-like state at the bottom of the pond. When spring arrives, the frogs reincarnate and the males sing for mates and the females drop eggs into the pond's shallow water, and the age-old cycle commences again.

Other frogs come to the ponds only to mate and lay their eggs. American toads, gray tree frogs, wood frogs, and spring peepers fall into this category. Once

Many dragonflies are associated with beaver ponds, the species composition varying geographically. American emeralds (bottom) are typical inhabitants of northeastern beaver ponds while blue dashers (top) frequent ponds in the southeast.

Skimmers are a dominant group of dragonflies at beaver ponds and their large-bodied nymphs are suited for life in still water. The group is diverse and contains (clockwise from top left): male common whitetail, female common whitetail, twelve-spotted skimmer, four-spotted skimmer, widow skimmer, and chalk-fronted skimmer.

(Bottom) Parasitic Arrenurus mites hitch rides on dragonfly nymphs about to leave the water, and then attach to the adults (here, a Halloween pennant) as they emerge from their nymph cases.

their metamorphosis from tadpole to frog is complete, they leave the water to return only when spring sends reproductive hormones surging through their veins. Older ponds may provide better habitats for the tadpoles of some of the boreal amphibians such as wood frogs; a higher amount of dissolved oxygen in the water has been given as one reason for this. Like those frogs, a few sala- manders, including blue-spotted and spotted, spend their youthful lives in the pond but as adults return only to mate and lay eggs. Red-spotted newts have a more complex lifestyle, often living in the ponds as gill-breathing adults

and spending their larval stage on land. The importance of beaver ponds as breeding habitat for amphibians has been shown in many studies; in the Boreal Foothills of Alberta, beavers create more than 90 percent of the still- water habitat and, thus, play a particularly important role in the conservation of frogs in that area.

As soon as beavers block the flow of water and a pond is born, pioneering plants and animals start exploiting the new habitat. As time passes, the maturing pond supports a larger complement of living things. Ironically, the diversity of living things in the water stilled

Many species of frogs use beaver ponds for part or all of their life cycle. Some, such as (clockwise from top left) green frogs, mink frogs, and bullfrogs, remain in the pond after their tadpole stage is finished.

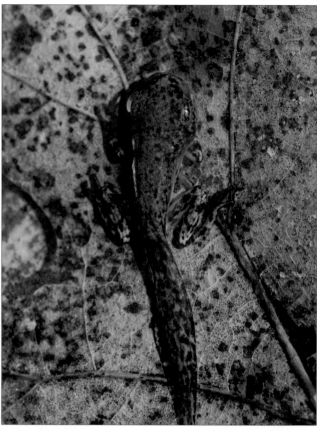

(Top left) Gray tree frogs leave their lofty perches to mate and lay their eggs in beaver ponds. (Top right) The spotted tail of the gray tree frog tadpole, which transforms into a land-dwelling adult in less than two months, provides camouflage when it rests over dead leaves lining the bottom of a pond.

(Bottom left) Leopard frogs sometimes remain near the water as adults, but they also disperse great distances, returning to the pond to mate or overwinter. Other amphibians, including American toads (bottom right) visit ponds only to reproduce. The males stake a territory and loudly proclaim their worth as a mate.

by the beavers starts to increase at the same time the lives of those being drowned by the rising water begins to fade.

When mating, male frogs and toads hold the females in a special grip called amplexus until they release their eggs, at which point the males release their sperm. This male American toad is quite literally holding his breath as he waits for that moment to arrive!

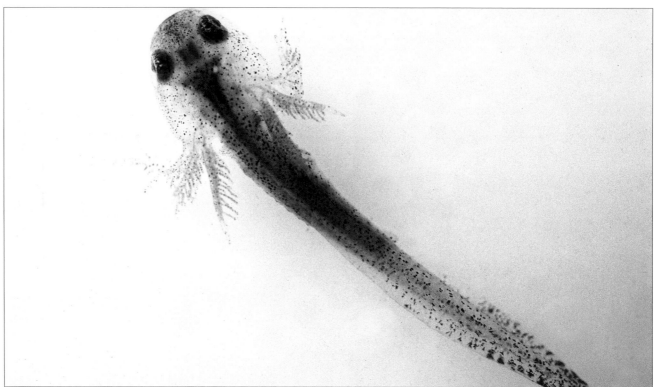

Spotted salamanders also use beaver ponds only for their egg and larval stages.

Smaller pond inhabitants are food for eastern ribbon snakes (top) and northern water snakes (bottom) whose keeled scales likely aid them in swimming.

(Top) Mink regularly patrol the shores of beaver ponds for frogs and other small animals and dive into the water for fish. This one was working an autumn food pile for minnows sheltering among the submerged branches.

(Bottom) The large whiskers known as vibrissae provide river otters with a developed tactile sense for finding food in murky waters. These aquatic weasels not only visit beaver ponds regularly, they also sometimes den in abandoned lodges.

(Top) Although they occasionally bask on logs, rocks, or even beaver lodges, most snapping turtles are seen only when crossing a dam or when females leave the pond to lay their eggs.

(Bottom) Blanding's turtles are rather reclusive inhabitants of smaller beaver ponds.

(Top) Hooded mergansers, here a female, are archetypal beaver pond ducks. These small diving ducks have narrow, serrated bills for grabbing small fish and large invertebrates.

(Bottom) Wood ducks, like hooded mergansers, nest in tree cavities but they are not diving ducks. Instead, they pluck food from the water's surface or the shallows, and harvest acorns on land.

(Top) The large bills of mallards allow them to filter food from material lifted from the bottom of a pond.

(Bottom) Beaver ponds are nothing less than duck factories. After mating, male American black ducks, like other ducks, abandon their mates, leaving them with all parental duties.

(Top) This red fox has just captured a nesting mallard and is bringing his prize to his mate in the den. The benefits of a beaver pond spread far beyond its boundaries.

(Bottom) A belted kingfisher surveys a pond for small fish, which it will catch by diving in headfirst.

174

In recent years, Canada geese have taken to beaver ponds and are especially fond of placing their nest on top of lodges.

(Top and bottom left) Eastern kingbirds, named for a fearless defence of their territory, exploit a pond's rich bounty of flying insects to satisfy the insatiable appetites of their young.

(Bottom right) Beaver ponds are active places at night. Raccoons use their touch-sensitive paws to locate food in the shallow water along the shore.

(Left) The long legs of a great blue heron allow it to stand in shallow water while it patiently waits for a frog, fish, or snake to make a fatal move.

(Below) At dusk, great horned owls visit beaver ponds to hunt for animals as large as muskrats.

CHAPTER 6

THE LIVING DEAD

elieved of its urgent journey, the water behind a new beaver dam rises slowly and gradually envelops the land. Trees, once part of a continuous forest growing atop solid ground, become isolated islands. As the roots gasp their final breaths, the trees' will to live fades, and their leaves wilt and drop. Conifer needles depart in a blaze of glory, flaming orange and red before they fall. On all trees, the bark and leafless branches linger for a while, but ultimately the years weaken their hold. Stripped of all garb and bleached by the sun, the naked trunks hold silent vigil until time takes them, too.

As their defences wane, the dying trees become inundated with insects. Bark beetles mine the wood just beneath the bark, creating spectacular mazes of tunnels as they feed. Metallic wood-boring beetles add their wider graffiti to the dead wood, and long-horned beetles dig deep pits as they dine. Spores of fungus, especially those of the woody bracket fungi, sprout in crevices and holes, finding little resistance as their mycelial fingers probe the wood. Eventually, lacy lichens dangle from branches and encrust lifeless bark with coats painted grey, black, and green.

The wealth of living organisms does not go unnoticed. Nematode worms and the larvae of fungus beetles and fungus gnats devour the flesh of the mushrooms that sprout from the trees. Wood-boring beetle grubs attract the attention of ichneumon wasps, which deposit their eggs on the insects after chemically burning a hole through the wood. Woodpeckers vie for the same larvae, plucking them out of their hidden recesses with their extensible tongues. These creative birds clearly demonstrate that there is more than one way to exhume a grub. Hairy and downy woodpeckers drill small holes to access the insects. Black-backed and American three-toed woodpeckers strip off the bark to reach their quarry, which is usually bark beetles lying in their galleries. Pileated woodpeckers spare no effort when they find a colony of carpenter ants, their massive excavations reaching into the heart of the tree.

Woodpeckers are not the only birds to find invertebrate meals in the drowned trees. Creepers spiral up the trunks, their thin curved beaks plucking tasty prizes from under the bark. Nuthatches go about their business while hanging upside down, and chickadees tear apart punkie wood and flip up moss and loose bark as they search for food.

For many of these birds the dead trees also provide lodging. Brown creepers hide their fine twig nests under

chunks of loose bark, while flickers and black-backed woodpeckers excavate homes in the wood. After the young have fledged and a nesting cavity is abandoned, it is never long before some other creature claims squatter's rights. The waiting list is long: tree swallows, great crested flycatchers, white-breasted nuthatches, prothonotary warblers, European starlings, bluebirds, and small owls, including northern saw-whet, boreal, and screech-owls, all have their names etched on it. A lack of true wings does not keep flying squirrels from exploiting an unclaimed hole, and larger openings attract the attention of common grackles, wood ducks, hooded mergansers, and common goldeneyes. Relatively large predatory birds—American kestrels, barred owls, and northern hawk owls—covet more spacious chambers, too.

Surrounded by water, the drowned trees offer safe haven to birds that build their nests not in cavities, but exposed to the elements. As they incubate their eggs, eastern kingbirds look out over the water. From their elevated platforms, great blue herons enjoy a more panoramic view. These birds seldom nest alone, and in some ponds, dozens of nests adorn the trees. In large

heronries, a near-deafening cacophony of screams, rattles, and grunts erupts when the parents return with food. Heron nests are seemingly flimsy, appearing as if the birds were rushed in their building efforts, with time available only for throwing a few sticks together. More substantial are the nests of ospreys, fish-eating hawks that reuse the same nest, as do herons, as long as the tree remains standing. Before either of these large birds returns in the spring, great horned owls occasionally usurp one of their nests. Seemingly more brazen, common grackles sometimes place their nest inside the tangled branches of an active heron or osprey nest.

The dead trees provide another service for birds of prey. Their height and lack of view-obstructing vegetation make them exceptional vantage points from which to hunt. In many regions the seasons see a changing of the

A new dam quickly raises the water level, flooding roots and drowning trees. Dying conifers go out in a blaze of glory.

guard; the lofty summer perches of red-shouldered and broad-winged hawks become the winter watchtowers of northern shrikes and great gray owls.

Even after they grow weary of standing, dead trees continue to play important roles in the pond ecosystem. Soon after they are reduced to logs, some floating, some solidly tied to the bottom, the trunks of the once mighty wear a carpet of moss. In thick hummocks of sphagnum, moist from water wicked from the pond, female four-toed salamanders lay and guard their eggs. The logs support a plethora of small plants, including delicate sundews that display a ravenous appetite for insects. Ducks, snakes, and turtles lounge on the fallen trunks, soaking up the sun's energy and ridding their bodies of parasites as they laze the hours away. Beavers also take advantage of the logs, using them as platforms on which they groom and dine in safety.

While their biological importance can be

Even in their death throes, trees still have much to offer to plants and animals. Bracket fungi (here, artist's conk) sprout on the trunks, their root-like mycelia probing the wood and breaking down its cellulose skeletons.

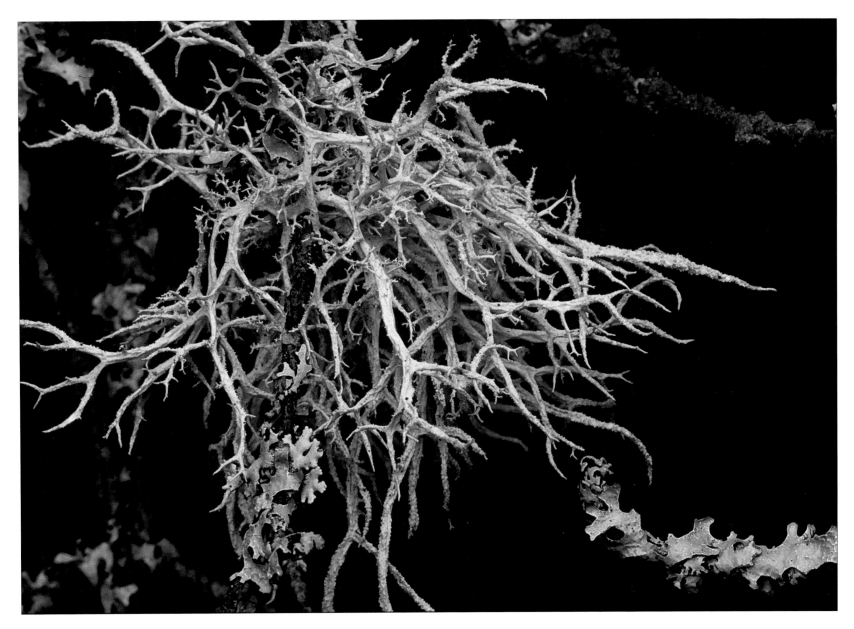

dissected and measured, dead trees also possess less tangible attributes. They exude a stark yet ethereal beauty that lends unique character to the ponds they grace. Stoic guardians, they keep watch over the beavers' domain, a cloak of moss and lichen testament to their resolve. Only at day's end, when the sun's warm rays gently kiss their weathered frames goodnight, is their guard relaxed. The next morning the seeming lifeless skeletons awaken, and once again become the living dead.

As beautiful as any wildflower, arboreal lichens frequently adorn dead branches, using them as they glean water and nutrients from moist air and rain.

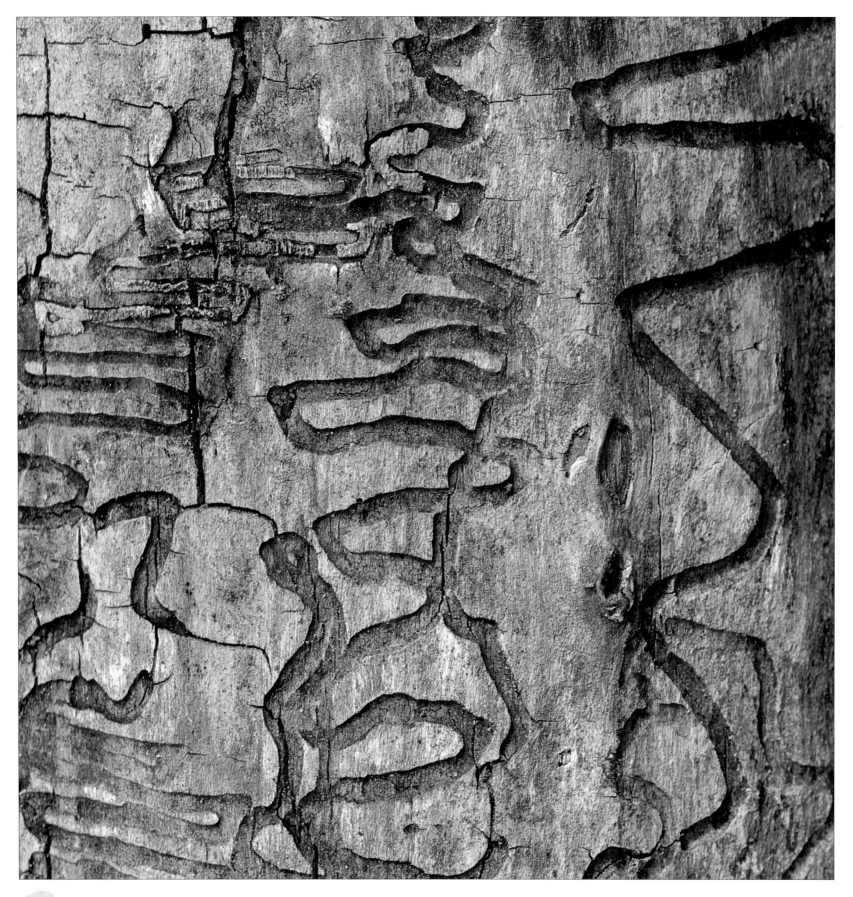

As the tree's defences wane, many types of insects, including jewel beetles (top left) and long-horned beetles (bottom), lay their eggs in the wood under the bark.

(Top right) The tiny grubs of elm bark beetles create the most beautiful patterns. The mother beetle, when laying eggs, created the vertical canal or gallery. After hatching, the larvae chewed canals at right angles to their mother's gallery and parallel to those of their siblings. As the larvae grew in size, their canals widened. Each canal ends in a chamber in which the transformation to adult beetles took place. Finally, the new adults exited the tree through tunnels and chewed to the surface of the bark.

(Opposite) When bark falls off dead trees, the artistic endeavours of beetle grubs are revealed. As they dine on the wood, jewel beetle grubs, also known as flat-headed borers, create shallow, wide-meandering tunnels.

(Right) Northern flickers are archetypal beaver pond inhabitants, excavating nest cavities later used by many other animals.

(Left) Once vacant, woodpecker nest sites are quickly usurped by cavity adopters such as tree swallows.

Wood-boring beetles are food for black-backed woodpeckers, which strip off the bark to access their meals. These northern woodpeckers use both dead and live trees for nesting, often those in or adjacent to a beaver pond.

The list of cavity adopters is long and includes (opposite) eastern bluebirds and great crested flycatchers. Small owls such as northern saw-whet owls (right) also nest in cavities, and nocturnal gray tree frogs (left) sometimes hide in them during the day.

Larger cavities house the nests of common grackles, which commonly bring back dragonfly nymphs and frogs to their hungry babies.

Ospreys (bottom right) and great blue herons (top right) decorate dead trees in beaver ponds with their nests, which become more substantial with yearly additions of material, which herons carry in their bills (left).

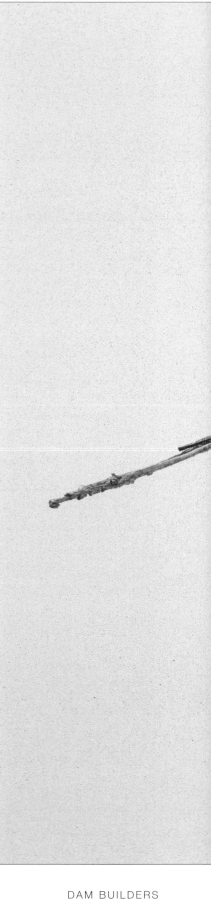

Larger predators such as red-tailed hawks (top) and great gray owls (right) perch in dead trees as they search for prey.

(Bottom) The branches of dead trees offer excellent vantage points for olive-sided flycatchers to search for flying insects.

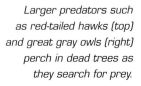

(Top) When dead trees finally succumb to gravity, their carcasses continue to provide important opportunities for plants and animals.

(Bottom) Painted turtles regularly bask on logs, using the sun to raise their body temperature and relax the grip of ectoparasites such as leeches.

(Opposite) One is never aware of the formidable gauntlet created by orb weaver webs in beaver ponds until late summer early morning dew reveals their presence.

Many waterfowl, including American black ducks (top), use logs as grooming salons.

(Right) Through time, fallen dead trees become nurse logs for a number of plants, including carnivorous round-leaved sundews.

DAM BUILDERS

CHAPTER 7
THE BIG FREEZE

Through autumn, beavers in northern regions become increasingly day-active as they prepare for the onslaught of winter. Extensive tree cutting occurs and while some branches might be used as building materials for the lodge and dam, it is primarily the quest for food that compels beavers to fell towering trees. The bark and twigs are what a beaver craves, and at the top of its shopping list reside poplars (especially trembling aspen) and willows, with white birch and dogwoods also favoured items. As preferred foods become depleted, beavers turn to those that offer less nutrition. It has been found that red maples contain a lot of phenols, powerful defensive compounds, and are generally not eaten as fresh food. However, by leaving red maple branches untouched in the water for several days or more, some of the chemicals leach out and the bark becomes more palatable. This food conditioning may be true for most types of trees, and as branches in a beaver's winter food cache stay submerged for weeks, even months, less palatable items may well become more edible as winter wears on. Conifers are generally avoided at all times because most are loaded with defensive resins and provide very little food value. Consumption of conifers often reflects a lack of choice or desperation; it is an indication of tough times

when beavers begin barking off the wrong trees.

It has often been stated that speckled alder is one of the most important foods for beavers. That notion is easily conjured when one examines a beaver's winter stash in northern regions. There, alder branches often adorn much of the visible food pile, which is sometimes called a "raft" because it floats until the branches become

(Opposite) The two routes taken by beavers from the lodge can be seen in this photo. The one to the front left of the lodge leads to the food pile while one on the far right leads to the shore.

(Above) With the arrival of the fall colours comes an escalation in beaver activity.

waterlogged. However, it is the uppermost portion of the cache that becomes locked in ice and therefore unavailable to the beavers in winter. The bulk of the cache, hidden from view, extends beneath the ice to the bottom of the pond and thus remains accessible. It is in the submerged part of the food pile that the choice foods such as poplar branches are, by no coincidence, found. I think it safe to say you cannot judge a book or a beaver's food pile by its cover.

The branches of alder and other less-favoured species often play the role of ballast in keeping the preferred foods submerged until ice coats the pond.

As autumn progresses, beavers continue to harvest food well into the day. Note the ice adorning this sweet-gale.

Alders usually grow prolifically along the water's edge, so by harvesting them, beavers conserve energy—less distance is travelled to attain plants that grow near the shore—and face less danger of being caught by a predator because they remain close to the safety of the water.

There are other signs that the upper portion of the food pile is of lesser importance to beavers. Debarked sticks, the inedible bones of past meals, often adorn this part of the cache. On numerous occasions I have seen beavers, upon finishing a meal, place the newly enjoyed branches on the top of the pile. They also add these items to dams. And even more often, I have watched beavers

(Left) A steady stream of mud and sticks is added to insulate a lodge being used during the winter. Note the double-carry!

(Bottom left) Sticks are not haphazardly dropped onto a lodge. Beavers perform frequent adjustments until they are satisfied with the placement of materials.

(Bottom right) Insulating a lodge is dirty work, but beavers never shirk their duties.

returning from foraging excursions dive with branches of poplars and other edible trees, sometimes with considerable effort, to add them to the bottom of the pile. While alder bark is occasionally eaten, especially in late winter, those northern shrubs play more important roles in the lives of beavers by providing easy-to-attain, low-risk building materials.

Food piles swell with a steady influx of branches, and lodges grow greasy as load after load of insulating mud is dropped atop them. The first freeze-up seldom slows beavers down and instead inspires a frantic burst of activity. Rather than wait for the morning sun to melt the ice, the industrious animals sometimes break the ice

[Above and left] Adult beavers are incredibly strong and transport surprisingly large limbs, dragging them by their butt end.

[Opposite] The paths that beavers create when bringing branches back to the water are appropriately called "drag trails."

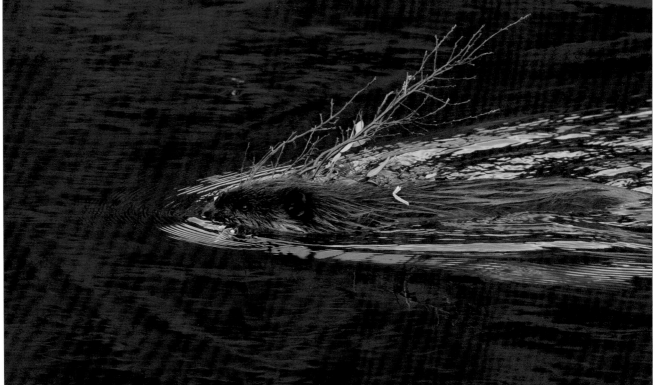

(Above) Less energy is expended when branches are pulled across water.

(Right) When the youngest colony members assist in building a food pile, they generally forage closer to the water's edge and bring back smaller loads than do the adults. Here, leatherleaf along with sweet-gale are being towed.

from beneath, using their powerful neck muscles and back of their heads to shatter the barrier. The first time I heard beavers smashing the ice, I thought a moose was unsuccessfully trying to walk across a frozen pond. Only when the ice forms a permanent seal does the frenzy of the autumn activity come fully to an end. As the ice forms over a pond, there are inevitably paths of thinner ice that extend from the lodge to the shore and the food pile. Even when most of the pond's ice becomes too thick to break, these routes remain open. And when they do finally freeze for the winter, they appear as grey highways winding through a white landscape—that is, until a blanket of snow cloaks the pond.

After watching beavers swim under one of those routes, I realized that there was more to the thin ice than meets the eye. When beavers swim underwater, a stream of bubbles escapes from their fur and nostrils.

(Above) The farther north a beaver lives, the earlier its food pile takes form. This food pile (with mountain maple branches visible) in northern Woodland Caribou Provincial Park, Ontario was already started by mid-July.

(Left) In northern regions, beavers create a cache of branches known as a food pile, which is located near the lodge. Beavers will wander some distance from the pond to retrieve choice foods, but the largest diameter trees are felled closer to the water's safety.

You cannot judge a book or a food pile by its cover. The top of the cache, which becomes locked in winter ice, typically contains less palatable items, such as speckled alder (top) or white cedar (bottom) branches. Debarked sticks are often found there, too. The uppermost material (sometimes called the "raft") serves as ballast to keep the choice foods below the reach of the ice.

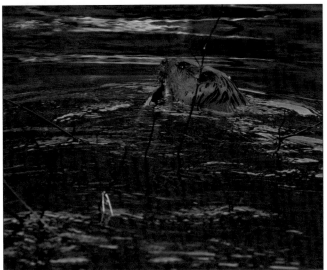

The bubbles rise and become locked in the ice as it slowly freezes downward. These bubbles weaken the ice, making it easier for beavers to keep it open. Thus, just like the underwater bubblers that keep paths through the ice open for ferries, beavers utilize their gaseous releases to help do the same. Early trappers were well aware of the ice bubble trail that marks a beaver's route, and they would look for this sign that told them where to break through the ice to lay their traps.

I love visiting beaver ponds in winter. During that season, there is a powerful ambience generated in part from the quiet still that dominates the cool crisp air. The silence encompassing a pond is neither ominous nor threatening; it embraces you in a gentle, comforting way,

(Top) Beavers residing near agricultural fields sometimes add corn stalks to their food piles.

(Bottom left and bottom right) Preferred foods are dragged down to the bottom of the food pile where they remain accessible all through winter.

(Top and bottom) This poplar log proved too large to be pulled under the surface "raft" so the beaver was forced to cut it in half while the log floated in the water. This difficult feat was eventually accomplished, and both halves of the log successfully delivered to their destination.

(Opposite) Trembling aspens are important components of many a food pile.

and makes you want to linger, often longer than you should, keeping you until shadows from the snags stretch cold blue across the pallid snow.

At first the silence might have you think that all life either has departed for warmer haunts or is hidden away in deep slumber. But you soon find evidence to the contrary. Tiny footprints set in pairs of two, with one set larger than the other, meander between the bases of snags. They reveal that under the illuminating stare of the moon, a deer mouse safely scampered across the snow. Not far beyond, you spot a near-straight trail of larger prints left by a red fox traversing the pond on its tireless quest for food, apparently unaware that a meal was so very close at hand.

(Above) This muskrat not only enjoyed the fruit of the beavers' efforts, it also co-inhabited their lodge.

(Right) As the days grow shorter and colder, food piles grow larger. The first hard frosts inspire a near-frantic pace of food storage.

In winter, the pond maintains a ledger of all who stroll, scamper, or lope across its frozen surface. It records comings and goings, pursuits and escapes, and the ultimate consummation of predator meeting prey. But as time passes, like old memories the stories fade away. Under the scrutiny of the sun, the edges of the imprints

(Above) When sub-zero temperatures coat a pond with ice, beaver activity keeps travel routes open.

(Right) This beaver seems to be tentatively testing the strength of what is very thin ice.

soften and lose definition. Playful winds swirl the snow across the pond, sculpting its surface and reconfiguring the tracks. And each fresh snowfall wipes clean the slate, erasing the records of the past while creating fresh pages on which new sagas will be written.

Animals visit beaver ponds in winter for a number of reasons. For many such as wolves, walking on the pond's level surface is easier than across hilly terrain. At times the wind-packed snow and thick ice allow much larger creatures passage. A beaver pond is nearly always part of a network of streams and other ponds, so for some animals such as otters it can be but a stop along the way.

At night, the snow-covered foliage of shoreline

(Above) Beavers break through thin ice by banging the back of their heads against it from beneath. Perhaps bubbles escaping from the beaver help keep the ice weaker and easier to break.

(Left) Here a beaver has been breaking through the ice to access a white birch log frozen in it.

conifers offers warm roosting sites for birds, and sheltered bedding places for larger animals. During the day, the bark and leaves of spruces, firs, and hemlocks provide chickadees and kinglets with invertebrate meals. Gray jays float in to retrieve their long-hidden caches from beneath loose bark and lichen clumps on the spruces. Red-breasted nuthatches and white-winged crossbills visit the conifers to rob the cones of their seeds. Because of dramatic fluctuations in the seed crop from year to year, ponds are alive with the chatter of birds in some winters and silent in others.

Snowshoe hares trample highways under the same balsam firs on which moose dine. White cedars attract hungry white-tailed deer. After years of intense feeding, all of the foliage from the ground to as high as the animals can reach is stripped from the trees. The resulting browse line gives the pond edge a manicured look.

In turn, the browsers draw lynx, coyotes, and

The upper portion of the food pile remains locked in ice all winter, which is the reason it usually consists of poor quality foods (here, staghorn sumac branches).

214

DAM BUILDERS

Beaver scent escaping from a lodge attracts the attention of wolves.

wolves to the pond. When a kill is made, more than just the victors benefit. Foxes, martens, and fishers, skilful hunters in their own right, join ravens, jays, and eagles in gleaning the smallest of scraps. Occasionally a beaver that has left the safety of its frozen world pays the price for such folly. But from its death comes life for a host of others; in Nature there is no waste.

Near the shore, the drowned trees provide wood-peckers with a wealth of food. Farther out in the pond, ice-locked snags offer superior vantage points for feathered hunters. From atop these lofty perches, northern shrikes and great gray owls monitor for the slightest rustle or movement; a shrew, vole, or mouse that dares to venture atop the snow often ends up as a meal. Even under the snow, the odds of escaping are only slightly improved when one of these hardy predators is on the lookout.

Warm air escaping through the "chimney" on top of an active lodge inevitably adorns it with hoar frost.

Hidden from view, animals come and go under the ice. Otters slip through the shallow waters in search of fish, crayfish, frogs, and other freshwater meals, including dormant turtles. In winter, these water wizards seldom remain long in any pond; their perpetual wanderings are chronicled when they belly slide across the snow and down shoreline hills and over dams.

Beavers also move around under the ice, albeit at a more leisurely pace. Leaving the lodge through an underwater exit, they swim to the food pile created the previous fall, chew off a branch, and return with it to dine in the comfort of their home. In lieu of branches, some beavers harvest the roots of water-lilies. As long as the food supply lasts and the water in the pond does not freeze to the bottom, beavers have a relatively easy winter. The impenetrable lodge keeps them safe from hungry predators and also relatively warm—when outside temperatures plunge to -20°C (-4°F) or colder, inside the lodge it remains a degree or two above freezing. But by late winter, perhaps because their food supply has dwindled, some beavers venture into the above-ice world. Whenever beavers emerge through a plunge hole or where the ice has melted back from the shore, it is always a nervous endeavour and their large noses work overtime to detect danger. With no small degree of expediency, cut limbs are dragged back to the safety of water.

When I have observed beavers foraging in late winter, their activity on sunny days often began in late afternoon, while on heavily overcast days, the beavers emerged much earlier. Perhaps the lower level of light gives beavers a sense of security. If so, it is sometimes a false one.

By February, thoughts other than sleep and food

occupy the minds of the adult beavers, and mating takes place in the water under the ice. Three months after mating has occurred, long after winter has departed the

By late winter, beavers running low on stored food create exit holes in the ice to access fresh food on land.

(Top) Counter-current heat exchangers in the base of the legs and tail keep those extremities from freezing in winter.

(Bottom) Beavers survive winter in relative comfort inside their lodge.

pond, the kits are born. Their first year will be one of leisure and unconcern, with even the arrival of autumn failing to inspire the urgency that inevitably envelops their parents.

On occasion, ponds become death traps for their inhabitants. If the water level is exceedingly low before freeze-up, or if the winter is exceptionally long and cold so that the ice becomes unusually thick, the water beneath can become depleted of oxygen. In this unusual situation, the larger gill-bearing residents can die from

Fur, blood, and entrails reveal that wolves came across a beaver outside the safety of its lodge. (Bottom) Eventually the author found the carcass, stashed under a log by one of the many scavengers that benefit from a kill. The scavenger's identity was eventually revealed when a red fox came to claim the carcass.

asphyxiation in startling numbers. More rarely, the water freezes all the way to the bottom. When this happens, all pond residents, including beavers, share the same unpleasant fate.

Spring eventually brings the inevitable end to the season of hardship. As winter passes, the sun grows stronger daily, its warmth soon freeing the ponds from their shackles of ice, and eventually the liberated water tumbles joyously over the dam. Beavers also regain their freedom, and eagerly return to their ageless commitment of maintaining dams and lodges, and seeking nourishment from the land.

In winter, moose (opposite) and white-tailed deer (top) often browse conifers along the edge of beaver ponds. Moose prefer balsam fir while deer devour white cedar.

(Bottom) Extensive browsing by deer results in a distinct feature called a browse line.

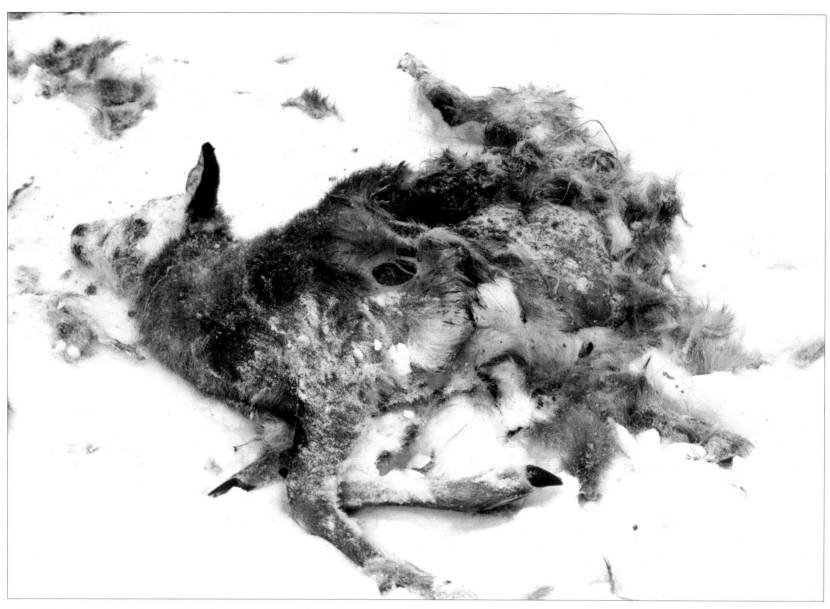

(Top) In winter, wolves often encounter their favourite prey in the vicinity of beaver ponds. Travelling over beaver-inhabited waterways offers an additional benefit for those social carnivores: walking is usually easier than through the forest because of the level terrain and wind-packed snow.

(Bottom) Nothing is wasted in Nature. Common ravens and bald eagles are among the many that benefit from the actions of wolves.

(Top left) Mink remain active all winter, leaving their tracks on snow-covered ponds as they search for food.

(Bottom left) Otters often adorn winter ponds with their tracks and distinctive tobogganing trails. (Bottom right) Where open water near a dam or fast current resides, these aquatic weasels bring bullheads and other meals onto the ice to dine. (Top right) The author observed an otter bring these young painted turtles (one at a time) onto the ice where it noisily crunched through their shells.

(Top) The late winter sun liberates beaver ponds from their shackles of ice, providing beavers with access to undoubtedly greatly enjoyed fresh food.

(Bottom) Adult beavers mate in late winter but the act is seldom observed for it takes place underwater.

(Top) Like other pond inhabitants, muskrats take advantage of the receding ice, using it as a table for dining and grooming.

(Bottom left) An excessively long and cold winter coupled with very little snowfall resulted in thick and slow-to-melt ice. This coupled with a lack of water in the pond resulted in a mass die-off of bullheads due to anoxia. Beavers also perish when the ice extends to the bottom of their pond.

(Bottom right) Hooded mergansers are among the first ducks to return in spring, often before the ice is fully gone from beaver ponds. Females garner a lot of attention from the males, which quickly vanish after mating. This one is obviously a real crest raiser!

CHAPTER 8

THE AFTERLIFE

The sole item that keeps a pond from becoming an empty basin is the physical integrity of the dam. If not kept in good repair, that structure eventually succumbs to the will of the water it holds back. Lack of maintenance usually means a lack of beavers, and this can occur through a number of processes. If the food supply becomes depleted, beavers abandon the pond. The death of the colony due to natural predators, man, or, in rare events, disease such as tularaemia also results in a beaver-less pond. Even well-maintained dams can break under the relentless pressure of surging water. A fast spring thaw on the tail of a winter dominated by deep snow, or a prolonged period of torrential rain does occasionally result in a breached dam.

A vanishing pond soon grabs the attention of predatory animals. Raccoons, mink, and a host of birds, including great blue herons and American crows are drawn to the isolated pools of water that house the remaining tadpoles, frogs, dragonfly nymphs, and small fish. As the pools shrink, their prisoners become increasingly exposed to danger. Inevitably, none escapes the slaughter. As the water recedes, the vast bed of newly exposed mud attracts American robins and killdeer and other sandpipers that devour the invertebrates that

wriggle helplessly in the muck.

The former bottom of the pond now exposed to the air pungently proclaims its liberation. Its rich organic content becomes inundated with oxygen-loving bacteria, and nitrogen, phosphorus, and other locked-up nutrients are soon transformed into biological fertilizer. The rich virgin soil soon sprouts green growth, arriving from seeds either carried by the wind or lying dormant in the bottom of the pond, patiently waiting for this opportunity to arise. If the former pond was in existence for only a

(Above) After days of torrential rain, this old dam succumbed to the inexorable force of the water.

(Opposite) Even after its water is gone, a beaver pond continues to provide habitat for a wealth of living things. The long-abandoned lodge is visible in the back right corner of the meadow.

brief time, the return of the new habitat to its state prior to beaver occupancy might take but a few years. But if the pond stood strong for decades, its transformation back to the original forest might never be completely realized.

Sedges and grasses are usually the first to take advantage of the organic bounty. Lush green carpets quickly form and, as succession progresses, larger and more robust species mingle with the colonizers. Wild-flowers peer from over the sedges and, through time, Joe-pye weed pink, gentian blue, boneset white, and gold-enrod yellow transform the meadow into a living Monet.

As the pond drains, the reign of the aquatic plants comes to an end.

What species of plants start growing in the meadow depends on several factors, such as the proximity of a seed source, the types of seeds lying dormant in the pond sediments, the pond's longevity (ponds that were resident for decades leave behind a greater thickness of organic deposits but these may contain fewer viable seeds), and the abiotic factors of the local environment (water and soil pH, temperature, amount of rainfall, etc.). Regardless of what species of flower-bearing plants appear, their colourful blooms inevitably attract a host of butterflies that dance across the meadow on painted wings.

The mud-rimmed pools of remnant water contain an ever-increasing concentration of imprisoned aquatic animals, copious bounty for raccoons and other predators. A robin's eggshell reveals that one raccoon likely found a bonus on its way to the smorgasbord.

It is not long before the rich organic muck, the former bottom of a pond, supports a lush carpet of sedges, grasses, and other plants.

As its name suggests, tussock sedge plays an important role in forming hummocks or tussocks.

Caterpillars, beetles, grasshoppers, and other insect grazers savour the rich bouquet, but not for its beauty—each species of plant is food for a specific regime of insects. And where there is prey, there are predators. The small herbivores fuel the appetites of praying mantises, crab spiders, assassin bugs, leopard frogs, and short-tailed shrews, to name but a few. Larger creatures, including meadow jumping mice, meadow voles, common yellowthroats, and savannah sparrows move into the meadow. The open grassland and its bounty attract weasels and foxes. Coyotes and wolves use these sites as summer retreats for their pups. Under the cool blanket of autumn, mighty moose perform their ageless mating rituals through the night and into the early morn.

Eventually, alders, willows, winterberry, and other shrubs find suitable sites to take hold, adding to

Sedges are a diverse group that possess subtle beauty. (Clockwise from top left) Nodding sedge, hop sedge, and bristly sedge are but a few of the many other species found in beaver meadows.

232

the meadow's heterogeneity. In response, the diversity of birds increases. Species from the nearby forest take advantage of the foraging opportunities offered by the meadow while others, such as alder flycatchers, nest in it as well. As time passes, conifers that don't mind having their feet wet—white cedar, larch, and black spruce—start to invade. As the decades pass, generations of plants add their remains to the soil, which grows thicker and becomes drier as ensuing communities suck its moisture up their roots and send it airborne via their leaves. If conditions are suitable, sun-loving trees such as poplar and white birch take root, setting the stage for conifers such as spruces, firs, and even pines to add their evergreen spires to the stage. A century or so after the dam has given way, a fledgling forest might stand where beavers once swam.

Once drained of its water, a beaver pond is anything but a dead environment. Although the original inhabitants may have long disappeared, a whole new set of plants and animals live, die, and interact where a pond once lay. Terrestrial ecosystems continue to evolve through time— that is, of course, unless beavers return and once again

Grasses and, to a lesser extent, sedges are the main food of most skipper larvae, and thus beaver meadows support a diversity of these tiny butterflies. (Clockwise from top left) Peck's, least, long dash, and broad-winged skippers can be as challenging to identify as are their host food plants!

reset the ecological clock by building a dam. If one were to dig down through a beaver meadow, down through all of the organic muck and soil layers, right to the underlying bedrock, quite likely there would be evidence of a series of beaver-occupied habitats, each separated by meadow and possibly forest episodes.

Whatever fate awaits the locale—whether it reverts back to forested stream or meadow or pond—beavers will have indelibly left their mark. And as long as they inhabit this planet, these remarkable rodents will continue to provide opportunity for countless plants and animals, enriching our lives in the process.

(Opposite left) Baltimore checkerspots have been increasing in recent years because in addition to native turtleheads, their caterpillars now eat the non-native English plantain, which also grows in wet meadows.

(Opposite right) Smartweed moth caterpillars, like many caterpillars, have a diverse diet and devour not only leaves of smartweed but also those of other plants, including trees and shrubs such as this dogwood.

(Left) Sedges are the preferred food of the caterpillars of Virginia ctenucha moths.

The diverse group of insect grazers found in beaver meadows includes slender meadow katydids (opposite) and alder leaf beetles (above).

(Left) Not all grazers in a meadow are small!

(Top) Meadows are vibrant habitats painted with the hues of pink steeple-bush, yellow goldenrod, and many other colours of wildflowers.

(Bottom) Which plants grow in a meadow depends largely on the site's acidity and moisture level, soil temperature, length of growing season, and other environmental factors. Dense cotton-grass prefers northern, fen-like situations.

(Left) Blue flags like to have their feet wet so they grow in wetter portions of the meadow.

Perhaps because of that colour's appeal to bees, many meadow flowers are blue. Square-stemmed monkeyflower (top right) and common skullcap (bottom right) certainly fall into that category.

Another blue wildflower, closed gentian, requires a strong bee to pry open its petals to access the rewards hidden within.

Joe-pye-weed may be a common wildflower but it is certainly not a weed. This native plant is a favourite nectar source for many butterflies, including monarchs.

(Top left) Swamp milkweed is another popular nectar source, as these dun skippers would attest to.

(Top right) Boneset attracts many butterflies such as this Atlantis fritillary.

(Bottom left) Many types of skippers, such as this Delaware skipper nectaring on swamp thistle, can be encountered in beaver meadows.

(Bottom right) White admiral caterpillars dine on willow and poplar leaves, but as adult butterflies they are attracted to the nectar offered by meadow wildflowers such as broad-leaved meadowsweet.

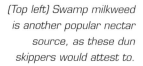

As long as there is water in or near a meadow, dragonflies will be found. White-faced (top right) and saffron-winged meadowhawks (top left) are named for their affinity for that habitat.

The abundance of small prey attracts predators. The beauty of damselflies such as eastern forktails (bottom right) and northern spreadwings (bottom left) masks deadly intent.

Different types of spiders hunt prey in different ways: (opposite) orb weavers build spectacular flight-intercept webs; (bottom left) crab spiders sit on flowers and ambush their meals; and (top) jumping spiders stalk their prey.

(Bottom right) Much harder to see are sac spiders hidden inside their nursery chambers made by tying down bent leaves.

(Top) Meadows attract more than insects; ruby-throated hummingbirds are particularly fond of the nectar held in orange jewelweed blooms.

(Bottom) This eastern wolf pup was part of a pack using a meadow as a rendezvous site.

(Top) Moose use beaver meadows for their autumn mating rituals. Cows call during the night and early morn to attract interested bulls, which irresistibly pay heed.

(Left) Frost adorns a moose's overnight bed.

Meadow voles are edible currency for almost every predator that visits a beaver meadow. Northern hawk owls, red foxes, and great gray owls (bottom right) are among many that provide a year-round assault.

(Opposite) Before they decay and add their nutrients to the soil, abandoned lodges serve as homes for small animals, including rodents and snakes, and occasionally even serve as winter dens for black bears.

Without further intervention by beavers, a meadow will eventually support shrubs like alders and, still later, conifers like spruces as it slowly returns to a forested state.

Northern creeks are inevitably adorned with both former and current signs of beaver residency.

CHAPTER 9

SUBTLE SIGNS AND CLEAR-CUT CLUES

So you come across a pond and you wonder if beavers are living in it. What do you look for? The beavers, obviously! But beavers are highly nocturnal and unless you are at the pond at sunrise or sunset, you will likely not see one even if they are present. But don't despair—there are indications of occupancy that can be looked for at any time of day.

A freshly cut stick protruding from a lodge or a dam, a chunk of yellow pond-lily rhizome floating on the water's surface, a pile of fresh mud pushed atop a rock—some of the clues of current occupancy are fairly easy to observe. Others, however, are more cryptic. And some—including a lodge or a dam—do not guarantee that beavers are currently in residence, for those structures could be relics from the past.

The following is a compilation of signs that tell you whether beavers are currently in residence at a site or have been there only in the past.

(Above) The growth of moss on the jagged end of the log reveals that this tree was felled a very long time ago.

(Opposite) Freshly felled trees and cut logs are sure signs of beaver presence, as is the recently conditioned dam in the background.

(Top) A speckled alder branch does not grow like this from the water. Conclusion: a beaver recently dragged it there.

(Bottom) Green vegetation growing all over a lodge reveals that it no longer houses beavers.

(Opposite) When wolf tracks converge on a winter lodge, it is a sure sign of beaver occupancy.

(Above) A complete lack of vegetation between the water's edge and the fringe
of conifers is a strong indication of long-term grazing by beavers.

(Left) Open water around a lodge and trails leading to it through the floating vegetation reveal beaver occupancy.

(Above) A skull lifelessly resting atop a bed of mosses is testament to wolves being one of the beaver's main predators.

(Right) The pointed ends of the felled white birch and its stump, the tooth imprints on those parts, and the wood chips on the ground tell us that beavers and not humans were responsible for this tree's fate.

(Opposite) The trail of thin ice leading from the lodge and debarked sticks frozen in the ice are clear signs that this lodge contains beavers.

DAM BUILDERS

(Above) A canal connecting to a muddy drag trail is a sign of recent beaver activity.

(Left) Flattened vegetation littered with debarked sticks near the water is evidence of beaver feeding activity. These sites are known as feeding beds.

A fresh pile of mud on the shore is proof that a beaver is present. If you smell the mud, you might catch a whiff of the beaver's castoreum, which is used to mark its territory.

(Above) Tracks are indisputable clues that beavers are nearby. (Right) The signs reveal that a beaver was dragging a branch on its left side as it waddled forward. The thicker squiggle to the right of the imprints of the huge hind feet was caused by the beaver's tail.

(Opposite) A red maple emerging from the water and changing colour prematurely is due to recent flooding that resulted from beaver activity.

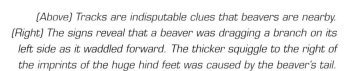

(Left) At first glance this lodge appears to be inactive due to lack of mud and other fresh signs. However, a newly cut stick (showing orange staining on the cut end) sticking out from the upper left of the lodge indicates otherwise.

(Top) Plants growing atop a collapsing lodge that lacks fresh material is a strong indication that beavers are not living in that structure.

(Bottom) Newly debarked sticks catch the morning light and glow brightly, catching the eye.

(Top) Beaver activity is visible from elevated vantage points. Open water above a dammed creek is a sign of current beaver activity.

(Bottom) "Donut" or "ring" bogs arise when beavers dam streams flowing through northern peatlands. The rising water floods the older, grounded portion of the peatland along the shore while the younger and thinner inner edge of the sphagnum mat continues to float atop the water.

There is no better evidence of beaver presence than the sight of one of these remarkable animals cutting its characteristic "V" across the water.

In autumn, fresh mud plastered on a lodge and a pile of branches lying alongside it are sure signs of beaver presence.

CHAPTER 10

THE BEAVER POND GALLERY

Beavers do more than create habitats and conserve water reserves. They create living galleries, ones that leave us with lasting memories of palettes of colour, subdued moods, and dramatic interludes. One comes away from a trip to a beaver pond with a wealth of memories.

The following is a small sample of the magnificent legacy of beavers and their ponds.

(Opposite) A beaver swims through the reflection of an autumn cliff.

(Right) Chips from a red oak reveal how a beaver worked the wood like a master carver.

(Top and bottom) Each beaver pond possesses unique and distinctive beauty.

(Opposite) Even under a blanket of snow, a beaver dam retains its character.

(Opposite) Raindrop ripples mimic the shapes
of the floating leaves of water-lilies.

(Top) Beauty beyond death; in late autumn the lifeless
stems of aquatic plants create a unique abstract.

(Bottom) Old beaver dams are soon decorated with
the blooms of plants such as orange jewelweed.

(Top) A pair of hooded mergansers swims into the embrace of a beaver pond.

(Bottom) Early morning mists mesmerizingly dance to greet the rising sun.

The first hard frosts transform ponds and meadows into stunning still lifes.

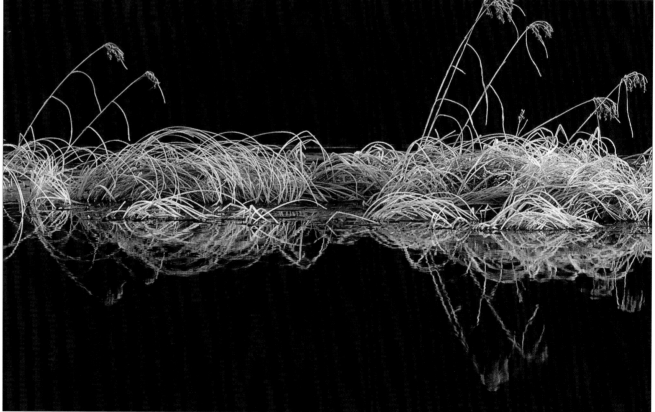

Frost-kissed alders (top) and woolgrass (bottom) reflections are but two of the many rewards awaiting those who visit a beaver pond in early morn.

On cold nights, the moist air emanating from a beaver dam invites the formation of hoar frost crystals.

(Top) A female wood duck explodes into flight, her mate poised to follow suit.

(Bottom) In order to get airborne, hooded mergansers run across the water.

(Opposite) No pond scene is complete without a beaver lodge.

(Left) Dead trees bring not only life but also profound beauty to a beaver pond.

(Top) Male wood ducks await the arrival of mates near an abandoned lodge.

(Bottom) Moose are regular visitors to northern beaver ponds.

In northeastern North America, the fall colours add dimensions of beauty to beaver ponds.

DAM BUILDERS

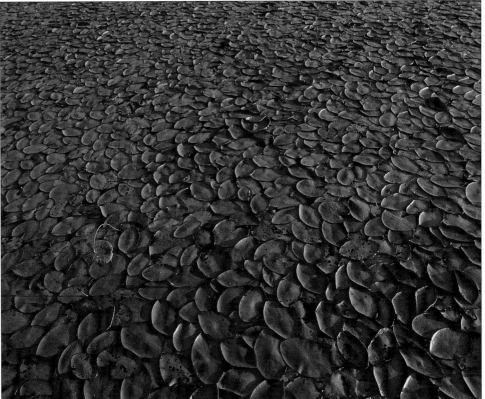

(Opposite) On misty morns, beaver ponds are mystical places.

(Top) Dead trees provide dramatic backdrops for moose visiting beaver ponds.

(Bottom) A water-shield tapestry.

Dead trees keep resolute
watch over beaver meadows.

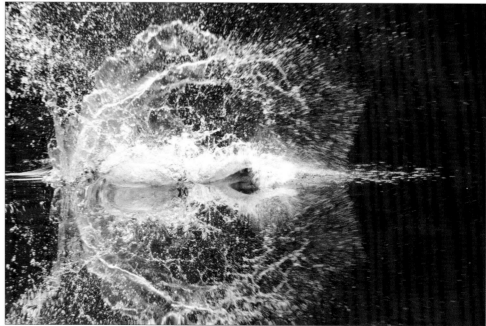

(Top) This water-lily leaf absorbed enough solar energy to keep the ice sufficiently wet to melt a light dusting of snow.

(Top and opposite bottom) A beaver's tail slap is living art.

(Top) A beaver enjoys a final meal before disappearing into its lodge for the day.

(Right) A pot of gold truly lies at the end of this rainbow.

ENDNOTES

There has been considerable scientific research conducted on beavers and their effects on the environment in recent years. The following is an extremely short list of select researchers whose work will provide you with more information on specific topics. Any of their publications will provide you with a trail of savoury crumbs that leads to other people who have conducted or currently conduct research in that field.

Evolution:

Natalia Rybczinski, Canadian Museum of Nature, Ottawa, Ontario

Castoreum and anal gland secretions:

Frank Rosell, Telemark University College, Bø, Norway

Eurasian beavers:

Duncan Halley, Norwegian Institute for Nature Research, Trondheim, Norway;

Howard Parker, Telemark University College, Bø, Norway;

Frank Rosell, Telemark University College, Bø, Norway

Food selection:

John Fryxell, University of Guelph, Guelph, Ontario

General behaviour and ecology:

Dietland Müller-Schwarze, State University of New York College of Environmental Science and Forestry, Syracuse, New York

Hydrological effects of beavers:

Glynnis Hood, University of Alberta, Edmonton, Alberta;

Cherie Westbrook, University of Saskatchewan, Saskatoon, Saskatchewan

EPILOGUE

Beavers are evolutionary wonders. They are complex creatures owning the power to create vitally important habitats in which a great number of other animals and plants live out their life and death dramas.

In our world, not the one in which beavers and other wild things roam but one in which its members are addicted to technology, we are increasingly losing touch with Nature. It is sad to think that many, if not most, of today's children have downloaded songs and images from the Internet and have texted uncountable messages on cell phones but have never been startled by the slap of a beaver's tail or mesmerized by mist gracefully dancing across a pond. They can name every character in *Transformers* or *Harry Potter* but cannot identify a single bird that perches atop a drowned tree. As the years pass by, fewer of our kind are having their lives enriched by direct contact with the real world.

Dragonflies and moose are not alone in benefiting from the presence of beavers. We, too, benefit, for the habitats they create will no doubt play essential roles in water conservation in regions affected by drought induced by climate change. And the habitats created by beavers indirectly give us a profound, less tangible benefit: they provide stimulation for all of our senses. Beaver ponds are living Sistine Chapels; they are Moonlight Sonatas. The magnificence of these living galleries stimulates our minds and enriches our souls.

Our world would unquestionably be poorer without beavers and their ponds. For our sake, as well as for the benefit of the many creatures that benefit from their presence, may the dam builders live long and prosper!

INDEX